Christian
Wisdom
of the
Jedi Masters

Christian Wisdom of the Jedi Masters

Dick Staub

JOSSEY-BASS
A Wiley Imprint
www.josseybass.com

Published by Jossey-Bass
A Wiley Imprint
989 Market Street, San Francisco, CA 94103-1741   www.josseybass.com

Jossey-Bass books and products are available through most bookstores. To contact Jossey-Bass directly call our Customer Care Department within the U.S. at 800-956-7739, outside the U.S. at 317-572-3986, or fax 317-572-4002.

Jossey-Bass also publishes its books in a variety of electronic formats. Some content that appears in print may not be available in electronic books.

Library of Congress Cataloging-in-Publication Data

Staub, Dick, date.
　　Christian wisdom of the Jedi masters / Dick Staub.—1st ed.
　　　　p. cm.
　　Includes bibliographical references.
　　ISBN 0-7879-7894-9 (alk. paper)
　　　　1. Christian youth—Religious life. 2. Star Wars films—Miscellanea. I. Title.
　　BV4531.3.S74 2005
　　248.4—dc22   2004027929

Printed in the United States of America
FIRST EDITION
HB Printing   10 9 8 7 6 5 4 3 2

CONTENTS

PART THREE
KNOWING 49

PART FOUR
FIGHTING 107

PART FIVE

SERVING 181

*To those before me: My parents, Dick and Esther Staub,
and those before them—Walter, Magdalene,
Cora, Arthur, and Etta.*

*To those after me: My children, Joshua (and wife Bonnie),
Jessica, Heidi, Molly, and those after them,
my grandchildren Mia and Eli, and the generations
of my lineage yet unborn.*

*To the one beside me: My wife,
Katherine Marie Wallace Staub.*

*To the Cloud of Unknowing: This cloud of witnesses,
pilgrims every one, contributed to my journey toward the
One to whom all my life and work is dedicated: God.*

ACKNOWLEDGMENTS

To journey without being changed is to be a nomad.
To change without journeying is to be a chameleon.
To journey and be transformed is to be a pilgrim.

—MARK NEPO

How did I become who I am, this bundle of beliefs and practices? Who bumped the trajectory of my life and spilled onto the pages of this small book? Let me say in advance this list is partial and I apologize to those whose imprint is deep on my life and yet go unmentioned (due to my advanced years and memory loss) in this cryptic list of acknowledgments. Those listed below (and where

I met them) are among the pilgrims with whom I have made my journey towards Understanding the Christian Wisdom of the Jedi Masters.

Fullerton: Jim and Mary Jane Sellers (Janis, Jimmy, Judy, Jennifer, and Jon), Bill and Joyce Siewert, Becky Reynolds, Ray and Ruth Brown, Neil Ramsey, George and Ruth Rennie, Zoe Parker, Earl Lemmon, Shawn Nolan, and my siblings Becky (Husband Phil), Ruthy (Husband Tommy), and Timmy. **San Francisco:** Don Kenyon, Russ Marshall, Tom Collard, Hugh Humphries, Earl Palmer, L. L. King, Ray Homan, Roger Kincaid, Dario Fraticelli, Mike Pickard, Case Verploegh, Sherri Sellers, Marcia Anderson, Caroline Berry, Loren and Charlene Brown, Nathan Bailey, Mark Lee, Peter Duda, Dale Dyke, Elizabeth Hough, Dick Bolles, Rick and Beverly Haight, Tim and Edie Owen, Nancy Beattie, Leron Heath, Don and Joy Kiehl, Danny Martin. **Massachusetts:** David and Jeanette Scholer, Bill Lane, Addison and Elizabeth Elliot Leitch, Doug and Jeannie Stuart, Bill and Myrtle Reid, Dave and Nancy Carlstrom, Paul Toms, Al and Alice Nanfelt, the Stewarts (Earl, Peggy, Mel, Bill), Ken and Connie Eckstrom, Gordon MacDonald, Wayne Anderson, Elmer Fitch, Mark and Linda Shepherd, Helmut Koester, Paul Toms, Harold Ockenga. **Chicago:** Lori Solyum, Cardinal Bernadin, Lee Strobel, Martin

Marty, Pete Hammond, Bob and Marty Briner, Jim Lemmon, David Neff, Scott Bolinger, Rich Buhler, Jim Rutz, Rich Gathro, Ron and Nancy Nyberg, John and Julia Dragstrem, David and Karen Mains, Mark and Gail Bailin, Tom and Lynn Futrell, Jerry Rose, Ray Pokorney, Alex and Pam Bolyanatz, Bob and Cindy Ward (Beth and Kaelan), Jahn Moskowitz, Mark Elfstrand, Scott Wilder, Mitch Bright, Dallas Willard, Jim Wallis, Ron Sider, Tony Compolo, Rich Mullins, Diane Quagliana, Steve and Kathy Wall, LT Reddick. **England:** Rev. John Stott, Bishop Stephen Neill, Nigel and Gillian Goodwin. **Belgium:** Luc Verlinden. **France:** Patrice Leguern. **Switzerland:** Eric Gay. **China:** House church members. **Indonesia:** Nanfelts, Kamphausens, Van Kurens, Rudds. **Greece:** Paul Sideropolous. **Scattle:** R.A. & Fern Harlan, Wayne Shabaz, George Otis, Ken Touryan, Ted Yamamori, Clarence and Rose Reimer, Ralph and Barb Mattson, Art and Nancy Miller, Gary Tailor, Gary Ginter, Mark Ritchie, Craig Roberts, Denny Mulder, Jeff Trautman, Ron Vander Grend, Bob Kraft, Brian Jennings, Ed Atsinger, Greg Anderson, Jack and Sheri Hoover, Matt Montzingo, Sam and Candace Vance, Scott and Pam Nolte, Doug and Jeannie Sutton, Richard Sterns, Atul Tandon, Paul Ingram, Bryan Zug, Jack and Alex McMillen, Luci Shaw, Gregory Wolfe, Jim and Paula

Mitchell, Greg and Kathy Strand, Doug and Katie Montzingo, Phill and Sybil Butler, Les and Leslie Parrott, Colin Greene, Davis Weyerhaueser, Hugh Maclellan, Elling and Barbara Halvorson, Mike and Judy Guerrero, Jack and Vicki Carney, Rich and Anna Parks, Doug and Erika Haub, Bob and Joy Drovdahl, Rand and Debbie Miller, Ron and Barb Miller, Bill Hogg, Brennan Manning. **The Lost Boys:** Josh Church, Mark Drovdahl, Ed Winkle, Jesse Stuart, Andrew Thwing. **Gifts of mercy:** Joe and Judy Rehfeld for the world's loveliest cabin getaway whenever I asked. Stan Mattson for arranging three days to write at The Kilns, C. S. Lewis's home in Oxford.

The pursuit of God in the company of these and so many other friends has enriched my life.

INTRODUCTION

Most men live lives of quiet desperation
and go to the grave with the song still in them.

—HENRY DAVID THOREAU

When I was young, songwriter Joni Mitchell warned me off the path most commonly traveled by my generation. In "The Arrangement," she describes a man who made regrettable choices and "could have been more" but instead settled for the always-needing-more lifestyle of a typical consumer, with a credit card and a high-prestige executive office. It is a choice that makes him want to die. She pleads with him that it is not too late to forge a brand new life.

There is no cause for sorrow like a wasted life, and our planet groans under a weight of sorrow; so many in my generation should have been more, their empty lives a warning to others. As for the next generation, you are full of hope, but are you sure you will find a better way?

Recently I was waiting in line for a Sprintburger at the Skagit Valley Speedway where the Dirt Cup Sprint Car races were about to be run under a hot, cloudless Northwest sky. A tattooed teenager stood in the midst of this crowd of hard-working, hard-living folks, looking as if he'd already had more than his fair share of disappointments. His eyes sent a message somewhere between defiance and defeat, and his T-shirt said the rest: "I'm like a superhero except without the special powers and motivation."

He wants to be more. He cannot bring himself to believe Tyler Durden, who said in *Fight Club*, "Listen up, maggots, you are not special. You are not a beautiful or unique snowflake. You're the same decaying organic matter as everything else." He is looking for a new mythology around which to order his life, and though he jokes about superheroes—and he would never admit it—he yearns for a heroic life to replace the one he is living. I know what he is looking for because it is a way passed on to me by my elders when I was just his age.

STAR WARS AND THE JEDI

When first we meet Luke Skywalker in the classic *Star Wars: Episode IV. A New Hope* (the first film released), he is not unlike our T-shirted boy in Skagit valley. Luke is a young man from a broken family who lives in the desolate desert regions of Tatooine, far from the galactic mainstream. Luke's life is stuck in neutral, helping his uncle Owen with the crops and repairing equipment, all the while instinctively believing his life is supposed to mean something more, hoping he is supposed to *be* somebody. He is "like a superhero except without the special powers and motivation."

The arrival of the robotic "droids" C-3PO and R2-D2 from space, and a subsequent encounter with the reclusive Jedi Obi-Wan Kenobi, changes Luke's life radically. Obi-Wan tells him about the Force, a natural and mystical energy field that both suffuses and binds the entire galaxy, and Luke discovers the Force is with him in exceptional ways. Obi-Wan enlightens Luke about Darth Vader, the personification of evil and a former

Jedi, whose anger, fear, and aggression made him a willing ally for the dark side and the Empire. A holographic message reveals Princess Leia Organa's imprisonment by Vader and outlines a secret schematic of the Death Star, providing clues about its vulnerabilities. The impulsive Luke is ready to spring into action, but instead by *Star Wars: Episode V. The Empire Strikes Back,* Kenobi has sent him to Yoda, a venerable Jedi master whose very existence ensures the rebirth of the nearly vanished Jedi knights. Yoda first helps Luke unlearn all he has been taught about what constitutes reality and then begins the lengthy process of instructing Luke in simple yet profound Jedi wisdom—a new mythology, if you will.

A myth is a story that confronts us with the big picture, something transcendent and eternal, and in so doing explains the worldview of a civilization. Luke Skywalker's life is transformed from quiet desperation to intense meaning when he finds a mentor who helps him identify his mission in the prevailing mythology. Until Obi-Wan and Yoda reveal spiritual realities to him, Luke is blinded to what matters most and sees only the insignificant details of the here-and-now; as a result something essential and deeply important is missing in his life.

In discovering the myth, the story in which he finds himself, Luke discovers his place in the story.

Myths usually unfold around similar themes: an unlikely individual is selected for an important mission, is mentored, and heads out on an epic journey in which there are severe tests and trials. Against insurmountable odds, and in the company of friends, the central character is transformed from everyman into a heroic figure. Think Luke Skywalker, Harry Potter, Frodo Baggins, Buffy the Vampire Slayer.

LookING FoR A YoDA

This book was born during a conversation with a young man named Ed, who described to me his desire to go deeper in his spiritual life as well as his uncertainty about how to make that happen. We had just seen the latest installment of the *Star Wars* prequels, so I restated his issue in that context: "It's like you want to be a 'Jedi Christian' and my generation didn't produce a Yoda."

I could tell what I said struck a nerve. Like so many in his generation, Ed was raised Christian (not surprising, since 77 percent of Americans still declare Christianity as their official religion) but was turned off by the Christianity he saw around him. Research shows there are four reasons the younger generation is leaving their Christian roots: (1) they never experienced God in their worship, (2) their tribal connections are stronger outside church than in it, (3) the issues being discussed at church don't matter to them and the issues that matter aren't being discussed, and (4) they didn't see anything compelling enough in their parents' lives to make them follow a similar path.

As we talked I realized that, like Luke Skywalker, Ed and his peers need a mentor, a clarity of mission, and a reintroduction to what C. S. Lewis and J.R.R. Tolkien called the "one true myth," Christianity. Luke Skywalker was unaware of the Force and unacquainted with the power of the Jedi because the ancient wisdom had skipped a few generations. Only by rediscovering ancient teachings from a Yoda who remembered them could Luke discover his true destiny. Likewise, the authentic Christianity I learned in my youth has all but disappeared; who can blame young people for abandoning the pathetic imposter that has taken its place?

The Chinese have a saying: "When the pupil is ready, the teacher will come." Luke found his Obi-Wan and Yoda, Harry found his Dumbledore, Frodo found his Gandalf, and Buffy found her Giles. Christianity is a prevailing myth of Western culture; Star Wars is a prevailing myth of our popular culture. The synergy of the two reveals Christian wisdom seen through the Jedi masters. If you are hungry to discover your true destiny and your place in the cosmic story, then be assured that there are those of us who remember the radical faith and are prepared to pass it on to you, as Yoda passed the Jedi ways on to Luke.

You now hold in your hands the secrets of spiritual knowledge, practice, and power, entrusted to me by "Jedi Christians" who have in succession and without fail passed on these sayings of earlier Christians since they were first revealed to humans by God.

For centuries these spiritual masters have conveyed deep spiritual truth from one generation to the next, entrusting it like a baton in a relay race, with each successive generation knowing theirs might be the one that drops the baton of truth, breaking the hitherto uninterrupted perpetuation of teachings whose worth is greater than gold and whose possession offers the path to spiritual joy and power.

In my lifetime the gravitational pull toward the dark side has been strong. Many Christians aspiring to Jedi-like wisdom have been compromised; others have gone into hiding. Though my embodiment of the truths I am about to reveal is flawed, I pray my first-hand observations of the most powerful and excellent masters, and my tutelage under their wise and holy ways, will be adequate to spark a next generation of Christians to surpass mine, and perhaps match or exceed the wisdom and power of the generations that went before me.

The ways of the masters must be rediscovered and brought back to life in your generation; if not, I fear they may be lost forever to the eternal detriment of all who do now or someday will inhabit this planet.

Consume this journal of remembrances at your own risk. It contains the greatest of hopes for an adventuresome life in the spirit, and it carries the potential burden of disappointment that I now bear in knowing what once was and again could be but was nearly lost in my generation.

Introduction

Christian
Wisdom
of the
Jedi Masters

Part 1

THE LORD
of the
FORCE

CHAPTER 1

Lord of the Force

The Force will be with you . . . always!

—OBI-WAN KENOBI, TO LUKE SKYWALKER

(*STAR WARS: EPISODE IV. A NEW HOPE*)

Who then is this, that he commands even the
winds and the water, and they obey him?

—DISCIPLES, TO JESUS (LUKE 8:25)

One of *Star Wars'* great contributions to
contemporary belief is the reinforcement
of the centuries-old teaching, advanced by
all religions, that something mysteriously spiritual is at

work in the universe. *Star Wars* creator George Lucas named this phenomenon "the Force."

The Jedi seeks to master the use of the Force, to be suffused with and fueled by this potent energy that "surrounds us and penetrates us . . . [and] binds the galaxy together," according to Jedi Master Obi-Wan Kenobi. Yoda expands on Old Ben's teachings, describing the Force as a strong ally and source of power for the Jedi, but warning Luke Skywalker that this power exists in a delicate balance. Under pressure or in dire circumstances, strong emotions can surge: "Anger . . . fear . . . aggression. The dark side of the Force are they. Easily they flow, quick to join you in a fight. If once you start down the dark path, forever will it dominate your destiny, consume you it will, as it did Obi-Wan's apprentice."

The light-versus-dark dualism of Jedi lore parallels teachings found in Christian scripture. As early as the first century A.D. the Apostle John talked about "walking in the light" as Jesus is in the light and warned against having anything to do with the works of "darkness." The Judeo-Christian tradition tells stories of wonder workers such as Moses, Samson, David, and Elijah, who were so empowered by God that they worked wonders, parting the waters of the Red Sea and defeating a heavily armed giant with a slingshot and five smooth stones (in Star Wars terminology, they would be called "strong in the Force").

"Jedi Christians" believe that over and above the opposing forces of light and darkness there is a Lord over all, including the Force. These Christians call this Lord of the Force God. The first sentence of the book of their sayings (the Bible) reveals that in the beginning God created the heavens and the earth, an awesome proclamation of a God whose generative power holds the entire universe together. We can liken this, along with the Apostle Paul's teaching that "in Jesus all things hold together," to the Jedi idea of an energy field binding the galaxy together, but only if we recognize an important distinction. In Jedi mythology the highest good is achieved by balancing light and dark, whereas Christians believe the highest good is achieved when darkness is defeated. In this Christian lore, the dark side is not just the opposite of light, but an unequal opponent of God, the Lord of the Force.

You've seen this idea of a Lord presiding over the dualistic struggle in the movies based on J.R.R. Tolkien's *Lord of the Rings,* where there are many rings, but "one Ring to rule them all." Sauron and Gandalf represent the dark and light sides, but Tolkien's title reveals his Christian belief that above all the rings and all manner of powerful wizardry there is a Lord of the

Rings who rules over all, and who will bring history to a just and good conclusion. Tolkien said of his work, *"The Lord of the Rings* is a fundamentally religious and Catholic work. . . . It is about God, and his sole right to divine honour" despite the fact that "Sauron desired to be a God-King and was held to be this by his servants."

The idea of God is not foreign to George Lucas, who in an interview with Bill Moyers embraces mystery over certitude in his understanding of God: "I think there is a God. No question. What that God is or what we know about that God, I'm not sure. The one thing I know about life and about the human race is that we've always tried to construct some kind of context for the unknown. Even the cavemen thought they had it figured out. I would say that cavemen understood on a scale of about 1. Now we've made it up to 5. The only thing most people don't realize is the scale goes to 1 million."

Likewise, the Jedi type of Christian embraces divine mystery humbly, professing a similar modesty about our knowledge of God, who though personal and accessible is also surrounded by what one mystic called "the cloud of unknowing." The church father Augustine agreed: "If you should ask me what are the ways of God, I would tell you that the first is humility, the second is humility, and the third is still humility.

Not that there are no other precepts to give, but if humility does not precede all that we do, our efforts are fruitless." Even though Augustine agrees God is a mystery to us, he reinforces the Christian belief that the purpose of our being is wrapped up in seeking, knowing, and serving the Lord of the Force. Those who succeed in that quest will be exceptional, like the Yoda and Obi-Wan of Star Wars lore, strong in the Lord of the Force and equipped to do God's work in the world.

Aspiring Jedi Christian, you hold in your hands an endeavor of love; an attempt to recover the lost sayings of the Jedi, so to speak, in this Christian setting; selections from the collective wisdom of faithful fol lowers who for centuries have pursued the Lord of the Force. May the Lord of the Force be with you.

CHAPTER 2

The Lost Sayings

The Force?

—LUKE, TO OBI-WAN, THE FIRST TIME
HE HEARS THE PHRASE (*STAR WARS:
EPISODE IV. A NEW HOPE*)

All the people wept when they heard
the words of the law.

—NEHEMIAH 8:9 (THE CHILDREN
OF ISRAEL HEAR THEIR SCRIPTURES
READ FOR THE FIRST TIME)

After years of studying with Jedi masters to develop his knowledge and strength, Darth Vader knew the ways of the Force intimately, yet he turned to the dark side. His children were taken from him for their own protection, but their seclusion left them ignorant of the ways of the Force—so much so that when he met Obi-Wan, Luke Skywalker was completely unaware of the Force and his own extraordinary potential as a Jedi.

In succession throughout the centuries, each generation passes its wisdom on to the next. But if just one generation fails, then essential values, beliefs, and practices can be lost in a matter of years. In a recent example, the Makah Indian Tribe sued the U.S. government to protect its right to harpoon gray whales off the shore of the Olympic Peninsula in Washington State. The tribal leaders were concerned that if the next generation lost their traditional whaling skills, they would lose the essential ancestral knowledge and practices that had defined them as a people for centuries.

The lack of Yodas has resulted in such a loss for the next generation of aspiring Christians. Christianity is always just one generation away from extinction, because the life-giving presence of Jesus takes residence in humans one person at a time, and spiritual practices leading to his presence are passed on personally from one generation to the next.

You may have been raised in a completely irreligious home, like Douglas Coupland, who describes his experience in the book *Life After God*. Like many open-minded people, his dissatisfaction with his own life led him to explore God. He wrote, "Now, here is my secret. I tell it to you with an openness of heart that I doubt I shall ever achieve again, so I pray that you are in a quiet room as you hear these words. My secret is that I need God—I am sick and can no longer make it alone. I need God to help me give, because I no longer seem capable of giving; to help me be kind, as I no longer seem capable of kindness; to help me love, as I seem beyond able to love." Perhaps you are curious about the spiritual, or have connected with the Star Wars myth and want to see how it relates to Christianity—the mythology most widely accepted by Westerners as a way to understand life.

Then there are those of you who have been exposed to the profound faith of your ancestors, yet have rejected it. The Prodigal Son was such a person. He left his father's house only to recover his senses one day; he comes home to his father after what is described as a season of "wasting his life in riotous or self-indulgent living." Perhaps you are such a wan-

Christian Wisdom of the Jedi Masters

derer; this written reminder of the lost sayings of the Jedi within the Christian camp can reacquaint you with the wisdom that has been lost in your life.

Many more of you are curious about the ancient truths of Christianity because you were born into another religion, or a home with a nominally Christian identity where the ancestral knowledge and practices that defined Christians for generations were not taught. You are not so much rebellious as unaware, and as such you wish to explore these lost sayings with an open mind. Then there are those of you who know that in Christianity you've stumbled onto something good, true, and beautiful, but you somehow instinctively know there is a deeper, more spiritually satisfying path than what you are now experiencing and you desire to explore it.

Jedi wisdom for Christians has skipped a lot of people; it is not the first time this has happened with a religious tradition. There was an era in ancient history when the Jews lost the written sayings that had defined and energized their faith for generations. When the prophets Ezra and Nehemiah rediscovered the lost book, they read and explained it so that the people understood. When the people heard and understood the sayings, they wept, so profound was the impact of the truth upon their lives.

We live in a superficial age. We long for the depth and substance of a faith that is intellectually credible, spiritually vibrant, and morally and ethically consistent with what we intuitively know to be right. We long for a good, true, and beautiful spirituality. These lost sayings of the Jedi in a Christian context offer hope, new life, and love, but they also demand change. Once the Jews found their lost sayings, they grieved and confessed that they were guilty of displacing the one true God with other gods; they then worshipped the One who alone was worthy of their praise. This pattern of awareness accompanied by grief, and then by confession and praise, still holds today as we recover our true faith.

In the early 1970s I worked with students in Cambridge, Massachusetts. A young man named Hank decided to read the Bible, which for him was like discovering the lost Jedi sayings for the first time. As he read alone upstairs, I could hear him crying out, "Oh no!" Then a few minutes later the silence would be broken with another "Oh no!" Hank was almost overwhelmed as he saw how radically his life needed to change if he wanted to be a follower of Christ, because the lost sayings are a double-edged sword, shining a light toward the right path while simultaneously exposing the dark side's effects on our life.

So, aspiring Jedi, if all this change is required, why should you even consider risking the uncomfortable revelation of the oh-no experience? Because unlike the dark side, which ultimately offers only the oh-no epiphany, the lost sayings offer the wisdom of the ages and an entrance to the spiritual dimension you long for so deeply.

Part 2

SEEKING

CHAPTER 3

Believe

I don't . . . I don't believe it.

—LUKE, WHEN YODA LIFTS THE
STARFIGHTER FROM THE SWAMP (*STAR WARS:
EPISODE V. THE EMPIRE STRIKES BACK*)

I believe; help my unbelief.

—A FATHER, ASKING JESUS
TO HEAL HIS SON (MARK 9:24)

The universal longing for something more hints at the existence of a reality beyond the physical. Just like us, Luke Skywalker wants it. As a seeker, he wants to turn his sleepy life of quiet desperation into one that is alive, wide-awake, and full of adventure. When old Ben Kenobi reveals himself as the Jedi Obi-Wan, Luke is enticed by the newfound knowledge of the existence of the Force. But nothing matches his surge of excitement when early in his training he first feels the Force. Ben tells Luke, "That's good. You have taken your first step into a larger world." Luke's desire to go deeper in the Force cannot be fulfilled until he finds Yoda, the Jedi master who can reveal secrets, guide him toward his destiny, and unleash his potential in this larger, spiritual world.

As Yoda would say, pursuing one's destiny frustrating is. Yoda is not at all what Luke expects: a strange, bluish, big-eared, wizened little creature, not more than two feet tall, wearing a hooded robe like a monk's. He cuts an unlikely figure for a mystical sage. Yoda begins the training with simple exercises such as balancing rocks, but Luke's impatience and lack of concentration are obvious—his learning curve is steep and progress slow. In spite of his passion and zeal for discovery, Luke struggles through his training with Yoda. He senses the Force is real yet cannot seem to break through and master it for himself. Ready to give up is he.

Sooner or later spiritual seekers experience disillusionment because though *every* religion promises a better life to those who tap into the Force, it is not easily attained. The Buddha said, "Just as a candle cannot burn without fire, men cannot live without a spiritual life." The Chinese philosopher Lao-Tzu spoke of the Tao, an ultimate principle of the Universe. Jesus promises his followers "abundant" and "eternal life" refreshed by limitless springs of "living water." "The glory of God is man fully alive," said Irenaeus, a second-century bishop, teaching that Christ is the path to this life. We yearn to be fully alive, but what are we to do when, like young Skywalker, we can't seem to break through to this higher plane of existence? Give up? Look elsewhere?

Despite promising a better life, no religious tradition teaches that finding or learning to use the Force will be easy. Luke's struggle feels so overwhelming that he nearly quits. He finally taps into the Force, but only after understanding and fully embracing the preconditions for a successful spiritual journey.

You must believe the spiritual force exists and is available to you. The smuggler Han Solo is a widely traveled skeptic who says, "I've seen a lot of strange stuff, but I've never seen anything to make me believe there's one all-powerful force controlling everything. There's no mystical energy field that controls *my* destiny." Han embodies the lowest type of man depicted by Lao-Tzu: "When the highest type of men hear Tao, they diligently practice it. When the average type of men hear Tao, they half believe in it. When the lowest type of men hear Tao, they laugh heartily at it." The promise of spiritual fulfillment and energy is real, but it is available only to those who believe. Han will not experience the Force because he does not believe; he lacks the prerequisites for a successful spiritual journey.

Luke is a "believer" who reaches the critical and transformative point of unbelief while training with Yoda. When he cannot lift the crash-landed X-wing starfighter from the swamp, Luke gives up, saying, "You want the impossible." He then watches Yoda mystically lift the plane to the shore. Luke says, "I can't believe it." Yoda replies, "That is why you fail."

Centuries of wisdom literature teach us that spiritual energy is released only when paired with human belief. From birth our instinct is to believe in a larger, unseen, spiritual world. Many like Han laugh; others like Luke are tempted with disbelief. But most of us are like the father who sought healing for his son from Jesus and said, "I believe; help my unbelief."

Albert Schweitzer, a philosopher, medical missionary, and Nobel laureate, said, "The tragedy of life is what dies inside a man while he lives." Do not let the hunger for the larger world die, because without finding the spiritual world you will never truly live. You must believe in order to enter a larger world.

CHAPTER 4

"Do. Or Do Not. There Is No Try."

Do. Or do not. There is no try.

—YODA, TO LUKE (*STAR WARS:
EPISODE V. THE EMPIRE STRIKES BACK*)

And every one who hears these words of mine and
does not do them will be like a foolish man who built
his house upon the sand.

—JESUS (MATTHEW 7:26)

Entering the spiritual dimension requires more
than believing the Force exists and is available
to you; it requires a determination to finish
the quest you have started.

22

As part of Luke's training, Yoda challenges him to lift an X-wing starfighter from the swamp by "using the Force." Luke thinks it is impossible. At Yoda's urging, Luke consents to give it a try. Yoda responds sharply to those words by saying, "No! Try not. Do. Or do not. There is no try."

This leads us to another precondition for entering the larger world: your desire for a spiritual connection must be so intense that you will no longer just *try* to enter the spiritual dimension; you will *do it*.

G. K. Chesterton once said, "The Christian ideal has not been tried and found wanting; it has been found difficult and left untried." At least Luke Skywalker *tried* to do the difficult, which is more than most people do. "Giving it a try" is insufficient in our spiritual quest, because trying always assumes the possibility of giving up. To try something means to put it on trial, to test it or experiment with it. We try on clothes to see if they fit, we try a new shampoo to see if it gets our hair clean, we test-drive a car to see if we want to buy it. Trying is tentative; doing means "to deal with for good and all; to finish up."

The laws of the spiritual universe require an intensity of belief that goes beyond trying. We must literally take a step of faith, to fully invest ourselves in this quest of finding and following God. We must leap off the diving board, not just dip our toe in the wading pool. True spiritual power is available to doers, not dabblers, to people who are deeply resolved to find God, not to people merely "checking their God options." This is what we see in all the great spiritual traditions. In the Torah we read the story of Jacob, who "wrestles with a man" all night and will not let go until he "receives the blessing." The struggle was so fierce that Jacob limped the next day, and he concluded that the "man" was actually God "face to face," who had tested then blessed his life. Buddha's quest involved a profound unification of the self and consciousness that bound them together as one. A sister tradition is yoga. The word is derived from the verb *yuj*, "to yoke" or "to bind together inseparably." Jesus says happiness comes only to those who "deny themselves," who "hunger and thirst" after righteousness and are "doers, not just hearers" of his words.

In today's superficial, fast-food age, we risk bringing a "hearer's only" shallowness to our spiritual search, but such a trivial quest is doomed to fail, because finding God requires going deep. In the story of the loaves and fishes, Jesus feeds the five thousand and the size of the crowd increases, but when he ups the ante by teaching that he will suffer and die, many disciples turn away and desert him. Jesus turns to the Twelve and asks, "Are you going to leave too?" Peter, who knows his physical hunger can be satisfied with bread readily available in the market, yearns for the "bread of life," real spiritual satisfaction. He is determined to stay with the one who can escort him into the spiritual dimension, so he cries, "Lord, where would we go? You alone have the words that give eternal life. We believe them and we know you are the Holy One of God." Such is the cry of the sincere spiritual seeker: *I cannot leave the path I am on; there is no turning back, whatever the cost.*

This is reminiscent of an incident in 1519, when Hernán Cortés's Spanish fleet set sail on a do or die mission. The sailors landed on the eastern shore of Mexico with big dreams, but after facing severe obstacles they became restless and wanted to sail home. Cortés commanded them to burn the boats, because he had no intention of leaving and he demanded the same from his followers. The sailors were "trying" life in Mexico, but for Cortés, there was no going back; he was determined to "do life in the new land" regardless of setbacks or the obstacles blocking his way.

In his final battle with Darth Vader, Luke reaches a place where the seriousness of his desire to master the Force is tested; he makes a decision to *do* it instead of *trying* it, and the Force is fully with him. After defeating Vader, he is tempted by the Emperor to turn to the dark side; Luke makes the decision for which he has spent a lifetime in preparation. Luke steps away from the fallen Vader, hurls his lightsaber away, and says, "Never! I'll never turn to the dark side. You've failed, Your Highness. I am a Jedi, like my father before me." In this pivotal moment, as Luke finds his resolve, the Force is harnessed, and the Jedi return.

What about you, aspiring Jedi? Are you ready to burn the boats and put everything on the line in your quest for the spiritual dimension? Do. Or do not. There is no try.

Christian Wisdom of the Jedi Masters

CHAPTER 5

Wake Up.
Be Healed.
Be Saved.

Help me, Obi-Wan Kenobi. You're my only hope.

—PRINCESS LEIA, IN HOLOGRAM
(*STAR WARS: EPISODE IV. A NEW HOPE*)

Except a man be born again,
he cannot see the kingdom of God.

—JESUS, TO THE RABBI NICODEMUS
(JOHN 3:3, KING JAMES VERSION)

Luke is cleaning R2-D2 when a fragment breaks loose, sending the boy tumbling head over heels. He sits up and sees a twelve-inch-tall, three-dimensional hologram of Leia Organa, the Rebel senator, being projected from the face of little R2. As the image flickers and jiggles in the dimly lit garage, Luke's mouth hangs open in awe. The image speaks: "Help me, Obi-Wan Kenobi. You're my only hope."

There comes a time when we realize the dark side holds us in its grip. Darth Vader captures Princess Leia and she calls out to Obi-Wan, because she needs to be rescued and he is the only one who can save her.

The spiritual masters use many metaphors for our condition prior to entering the spiritual dimension. They describe it is as if we are asleep, or blind, or born physically but need to be "born again" spiritually, or in bondage and need to "be saved." The dark side's effect on us is this spiritual obtuseness, making us violators of the spiritual dimension's laws. The Apostle John teaches that transgression of the law is sin and "whoever commits sin is the servant of sin."

The metaphors for our renewal all center on the importance of a new awareness, a moment when we awake from our sleep; we are healed of our blindness, born to the spiritual, and freed from our slavery. The process always begins with recognition and acknowledgment of our need, turning from our old way of life and dedicating ourselves to the new, and a deep changing of our mind about the true nature of our situation.

The first question Jesus asks of a sick man is, "What would you like me to do for you?" Isn't it obvious? He needs to be healed. However, what is more important is that the sick man know and acknowledge his need for healing. The implication? We can be asleep, blind, spiritually dead, or in bondage, and not even know or acknowledge it!

Only after recognizing our need can we enter the spiritual dimension; in the Christian story, calling on Jesus is the first step in our transformation. Jesus says, "Repent," which means to change our mind and our course of conduct. "Be not conformed to this world, but be *transformed* by the renewing of your mind." The word *transformed* is from the Greek root for *metamorphosis,* to completely change the nature of something, to change into a different form. The winter bulb becomes spring's colorful tulip; the frog, when kissed, becomes the prince. Applied to the spiritual journey, this indicates that a radically different person emerges from the process of awakening, healing, spiritual birth, and release from the dark side's captivity.

The twelfth-century mystic Hildegard von Bingen described this dynamic spiritual change as a work of God: "Giving life to all life, moving all creatures, root of all things, washing them clean, wiping out their mistakes, healing their wounds, you are our true life, luminous, wonderful, awakening the heart from its ancient sleep."

Today people sometimes talk glibly of their "spiritual journey" with little evidence of radical transformation. Such a person has not truly entered the spiritual dimension, because the spiritual journey is for those deeply aware of their need of transformation and wanting to be transformed. As the poet and spiritual writer Mark Nepo said, "To journey without being changed is to be a nomad. To change without journeying is to be a chameleon. To journey and be transformed is to be a pilgrim."

Pilgrims, aspiring Christians, wake up.
Be healed. Be saved.

CHAPTER 6

Seek First

You must unlearn what you learned.

—YODA, TO LUKE (*STAR WARS: EPISODE V.*
THE EMPIRE STRIKES BACK)

Seek first the kingdom of God.

—JESUS (MATTHEW 6:33, KING JAMES VERSION)

L uke Skywalker wanted to become a Jedi knight more than anything, but he didn't have the slightest clue how radically his life and values would change in his single-minded quest to become one. His entire being exuded passion, but he had no clear roadmap for getting there, and the skills he mastered in crop dusting on the farm didn't exactly equate to the spiritual practice necessary for advancement as a Jedi. He was a poster boy for zeal without knowledge.

The same is true when the aspiring Christian hears Jesus' command to "seek first the kingdom of God." Seeking God's kingdom involves submitting to the king as our first priority. The good news is that "if we seek we will find," but the frightening news is that we are invited to follow the King without knowing in advance where He plans to lead us!

To seek God's kingdom requires trust. That is why Jesus said it would be easier for a child to enter the kingdom than an adult. As adults we take little on faith because we have experienced the betrayal of trust, but children trust what they've seen and believe the rest will be as good or better. By the time Jesus called the disciples to leave their nets and follow him, they were skeptical adults, and the same is true of most aspiring Christians.

Unlearning your fear of trust is the first step in turning your life's direction to God. It is essential because you can't find God's kingdom without seeking it, you can't seek God's kingdom without trusting the King, and you can't trust the King without unlearning your fear!

Seeking God's kingdom first means that going deeper in the spiritual dimension is your strongest

Christian Wisdom of the Jedi Masters

desire. Prior to joining a monastery, Thomas Merton was walking on Sixth Avenue in New York City one spring evening with his dear friend Bob Lax, when Lax challenged him to trust God radically in his pursuit of the spiritual life. Lax asked, "What do you want to be anyway?" Merton replied, "I don't know; I guess what I want is to be a good Catholic." Lax corrected Merton, saying, "What do you mean, you want to be a good Catholic? What you should say is that you want to be a saint." Taken aback, Merton responded, "How do you expect me to become a saint? . . . I can't be a saint. I can't be a saint." Lax replied, "All that is necessary to be a saint is to want to be one. Don't you believe that God will make you what he created you to be if you consent to let Him do it? All you have to do is desire it."

Seeking first God's kingdom requires valuing the spiritual over the material. The late Jewish philosopher and theologian Abraham Heschel states this in the extreme: "God is of no importance unless He is of Supreme importance." Reorganizing life around God's supreme importance also requires "unlearning" our pattern of denying God's rightful place in our life. Jesus taught that a blessed person is the one who hungers and thirsts after righteousness. Jesus reminds us that clothing, food, and a place to sleep are secondary. This, of course, is exactly the opposite of the way most of us order our lives, and it goes a long way in explaining the leanness of our soul.

Today it is in vogue to talk about "finding the god within each of us," a concept that occupies the blurry limbo somewhere between misunderstanding, complete foolishness, and wishful thinking. Giving humans the benefit of the doubt, I'll call it a misunderstanding and summarize the situation the way mystery writer Nevada Barr did after her walk on the wild side and subsequent return to God: "It was a number of years of crashing and burning before I made the discovery that I was not God. . . . Finally I realized that though I was not God, I was *of* God."

Being of God means you are connected to God because He is your creator; you bear a resemblance to God because you are made in God's image; and because you were made for His pleasure, you now yearn for Him. This condition is the universal and collective experience of every human whether born in Boston, Bangladesh, Beijing, Buenos Aires, Berlin, or Botswana, and whether Buddhist, Christian, Muslim, or atheist. Though you are *of* God, you are not God; you will find your hunger for God within, but satisfying your spiritual appetite will take you outside yourself.

If you are wise you will devote yourself to seeking God and His Kingdom first, because only a deeper search leads to deeper satisfaction. Going through the motions of religious practice is not enough. As theologian Joan Chittister observes, "We see people die spiritually every day. Sometimes they look very religious in the doing of it, in fact. They go on believing, reading, praying, thinking what they have always thought. In the face of new questions, they dare no questions. At the brink of new insights, they want no insights. They want comfort and a guarantee of the kind of heaven they imagined as children. They think that to think anything else is unfaithful." You will never find deep spiritual satisfaction unless you move outside your comfort zone and make pursuing God's kingdom your life's deepest concern.

The twentieth century was characterized by the pursuit of earthly prosperity, and for most people, religion has coexisted with, been subservient to, or even championed that pursuit. The result is unparalleled material abundance coupled with profound spiritual poverty. Jesus calls you to travel the road less taken, seeking the kingdom of God above all else, trusting your life into the care of the King, and investing your energy in an unwavering pursuit of the One who is only found and enjoyed when of supreme importance in your life.

Aspiring Christian, be reckless and passionate in your pursuit of God. Travel on the road less taken and you will not regret it, for only God can satisfy your soul.

CHAPTER 7

Will one Thing

A Jedi must have the deepest commitment,
the most serious mind.

—YODA (*STAR WARS: EPISODE I.*
THE PHANTOM MENACE)

Purity of heart is to will one thing.

—SØREN KIERKEGAARD

Yoda understood that a serious-minded, deep commitment was essential for the aspiring Jedi knight. It echoes the Danish philosopher Søren Kierkegaard's clarion call for the same single-mindedness from followers of Jesus.

Kierkegaard was disgusted with the Danish state church in the mid-1800s because it had lost its first love and forgotten the primacy of pursuing God. The church had no interest in self-denial, repentance for sin, or identification with the less fortunate in society, all of which Kierkegaard saw as central to following Jesus. The Danish state church chose superficiality and cultural acceptability over deep adherence to the Gospel; it was more interested in power and adopting the fashionable dress and ideas of the day than in exemplifying a countercultural call to transformation. Describing them as "silk and velvet priests," Kierkegaard chided the leaders of the church for pursuing the profit of Christianity, taking money for their service in the church while abandoning its essential teaching.

Writing in his journal that he found this patronizing and hypocritical, he said: "In the splendid Palace Chapel an imposing Court preacher, the chosen of the cultivated public, steps forward before a chosen circle of the fashionable and cultivated public and preaches emotionally on the text of the Apostle: 'God chose the mean and despised'—and nobody laughs!" In *The Fatherland,* Kierkegaard concluded sadly, "The human race in the course of time has taken the liberty of softening and softening Christianity until at last we have contrived to make it exactly the opposite of what it is in the New Testament."

As a thirty-year-old, in a book titled *Either/Or,* he articulated his belief that following Jesus requires a radical choice between the sensual and the spiritual. Four years later, he wrote *Purity of Heart Is to Will One Thing,* passionately developing the theme that a Christian's commitment proceeds from a pure heart and is revealed in an unwavering, singular devotion he described as "willing one thing."

Kierkegaard equates purity—encompassing both clarity and cleanliness—with the Christian's dedication to God, which is to be unsullied by any competing affections or intentions. Loving God requires knowing God deeply, and such intimacy with God leads to a complete merging of our human will with God's will. Jesus sought to do God's will each day and taught us to pray, "Thy will be done on earth as it is in heaven." Following Christ's example, the aspiring Christian's heart turns to God's will as the flower is drawn and bends toward the sun.

Kierkegaard's singularity of passion meant he was unable to conform to the "Christianity Lite" of the contemporary church of his day. His spirit rejected that culture's dalliance with sensual pursuits and social acceptability at all costs. Out of step with both church and culture, his was often a solitary journey, and he concluded a "pure heart willing one thing" is rare; Kierkegaard felt this so intensely that he dedicated *Purity of Heart* to "That Solitary Individual."

You may experience this same sense of isolation on your journey, but take courage. Though Jedi-like Christians are few, when we discover each other, nothing is more satisfying than our pursuit of God in the company of such friends. One time, while speaking to a crowd, Jesus was interrupted by someone with the news that his mother and brothers were outside and wanted a word with him. He replied, "Who is my mother and who are my brothers?" Pointing to his disciples, he said, "Here are my mother and my brothers, for whoever does the will of my Father in heaven is my brother and sister and mother." Jesus wasn't putting down the importance of his earthly family; he was celebrating the value of sojourners who shared his passion to learn and do God's will together.

To will one thing for the duration of life is especially rare. The commitment made in one's youth is often choked out over time by competing affections and the cares of this world. Recently I was reminded of this when Matt Montzingo, a young man from my church, died in a tragic accident at the age of twenty-five.

Everybody who knew him had a "Matt story." Exuberant, sweet, tenderhearted, wild, sincere, naïve, trusting, aggressive, thoughtful, impulsive, driven: Matt was a forceful and innovative presence. He took on our church's youth ministry when he was twenty, and within a month up to one hundred wild-eyed, mostly unchurched kids were packed into the youth building after the Shorewood High School games. He loved the Seattle music scene and facilitated promotion of new bands by setting up a recording studio called Ash Tray Productions to record new artists' demos at no charge. He loved Jesus completely, and that love was poured out on everybody he met.

I suspect most of you know a Matt. These are the go-to men and women in the emerging faith community—young, energetic, with a pure heart— who will one thing. Matt's reckless passion attracted kids and sometimes made parents run for cover. His example helped me remember, and not want to give up on, the optimism and hopefulness I possessed at his age and stage in life—the desire and hunger to change the world.

When I heard that Matt had died, the first thing that came to my mind was Kierkegaard's book, *Purity of Heart Is to Will One Thing*. I picked up my copy and it fell open to a remarkable prayer aimed at young and old Christians: "Oh, Thou that giveth both the beginning and the completion, may Thou early, at the dawn of day, give to the young man the resolution to will one thing. As the day wanes, may Thou give to the old man a renewed remembrance of his first resolution; that the first may be like the last, the last like the first, in possession of a life that has willed only one thing."

Today's aspiring Jedi is turned off to hypocrisy and pomposity in the church and culture, just as Kierkegaard was. I'm encouraged by this development because it can fuel a passion and determination for the real thing in this generation, as it did in Kierkegaard's. The message is clear. Young Jedi, be passionate; "embrace the purity of heart that wills one thing." As for those of you in my generation? Return to the resolutions of your youth, return to your first love with an unequivocal determination to will one thing.

CHAPTER 8

The Seeker Is Sought

You're referring to the prophecy of the one
who will bring balance to the Force. . . .
You believe it's this boy? Bring him before us, then.

—MACE WINDU, TO QUI-GON JINN
(*STAR WARS: EPISODE I. THE PHANTOM MENACE*)

For the Son of Man came to seek out
and to save the lost.

—JESUS (LUKE 19:10)

U pon becoming aware of the Force, and seeing the work of the dark side in the murder
of his Uncle and Aunt, Luke Skywalker was
immediately eager to seek more knowledge, asking to
accompany Obi-Wan on his journey to the planet
Alderaan in order to learn the ways of this mystical
energy and become a Jedi. As the Chinese proverb
promises, when the pupil is ready the teacher will
come; Obi-Wan and eventually Yoda both responded
to the sincerity of Luke's initiative.

All spiritual traditions acknowledge the seeker's
journey toward the spiritual dimension, but a distin-
guishing and defining characteristic of the Christian
faith is the pursuit of the seeker by the Lord of the
Force. Yours is not a one-way quest toward becoming
a Jedi in Christian terms; the Lord of the Force is, and
has always been, seeking you.

The Christmas story relates how God, the Father,
runs to meet us. The manger scene heralds Jesus'
arrival on earth, but God physically sending His son
for our salvation proclaims the deeper truth that ultimately it is God who actively searches for spiritual
seekers. "God so loved the world that He sent his only
son into the world," or as *The Message* puts it, "the
Word became flesh and blood, and moved into the
neighborhood."

A central theme in many of Jesus' parables is God's search for the lost. An old woman has ten coins, loses one, and sweeps her floor looking for the one lost coin; a shepherd leaves the ninety-nine sheep and will not give up until he finds the one that is missing. Perhaps the most famous of these stories is the one of the prodigal son, in which a young man has taken his share of his father's estate, and after squandering his wealth in wild living he finally comes to his senses and heads home. Even in this story, the father, who has been watching for him, sees him while he is still far away, inspiring novelist Tobias Wolfe to describe these words as the most beautiful in the English language: "His father, when he saw him coming, ran to meet him."

Why is it important to know that the Lord of the Force is seeking you while you are seeking Him? The genuine seeker needs reassurance that though the dark side exploits diversions to inhibit our search for God, it cannot restrain the Lord of the Force from seeking us out. The light of God's love is too intense to be dimmed by the dark side. The old hymn encourages the seeker: "O the deep, deep love of Jesus, vast, unmeasured, boundless, free! Rolling as a mighty ocean, in its fullness over me! Underneath me, all around me, is the current of God's love!" God's pursuit is relentless, reminiscent of the Clannad song featured in the film *The Last of the Mohicans,* about one who will find us no matter where we go, even if it takes a thousand years.

Knowing that God is seeking the seeker helps us avoid the pride that comes with seeing ourselves as the noble and heroic character in the drama of the spiritual search. To believe that the primary search is ours, that we seek a God who is apparently indifferent toward us, implies that our love for God is somehow greater or deeper than His love for us.

Furthermore, even though some people sincerely seek God, often the last thing humans desire is to find or be found by God. C. S. Lewis, once an agnostic, astutely observed that "amiable agnostics will talk cheerfully about 'man's search for God.' To me, as I then was, they might as well have talked about the mouse's search for the cat!" This is why some people, though found by God, foolishly choose to remain with the dark side. Polls regularly indicate that more than 80 percent of Americans are spiritual seekers, yet is it possible that God has already sought and found many of these seekers, who, after given the chance to know God, choose to retain their autonomy rather than yield to the authority of the Lord of the Force?

Jesus promises that those who seek will find, because he knows God pursues and finds those who search for Him. In our fallenness we are sometimes blind to the God who is already here, but once seekers find God His presence is so obvious that they often wonder how they missed it for so long. The late theologian Catherine M. LaCugna puts it this way: "One finds God because one is already found by God. Anything we would find on our own would not be God."

The late Henri Nouwen came to this realization after years of struggling to know and find God and then described his radical change in outlook once he realized God had been trying to find, know, and love him all along. "The question is not, 'How am I to find God?' but 'How am I to let myself be found by him?' The question is not 'How am I to know God?' but 'How am I to let myself be known by God?' And, finally, the question is not 'How am I to love God?' but 'How am I to let myself be loved by God?'"

Aspiring Jedi, your success in seeking the Lord of the Force requires putting down your guard and allowing the Lord of the Force to find, know, and love you, just as you are.

Part 3

kNoWING

CHAPTER 9

Enter the Cloud of Unknowing

I've never seen anything to make me believe there's one all-powerful force controlling everything.

—HAN SOLO, TO LUKE,
WHEN OBI-WAN MENTIONS THE FORCE
(*STAR WARS: EPISODE IV. A NEW HOPE*)

No one has ever seen God.

—1 JOHN 4:12

In Jedi lore, the Force is everywhere and yet is unseen. The ways of the Force are beyond intellectual comprehension, but the Jedi devote all their energy and resources to understanding and mastering its ways. Luke Skywalker's life was forever changed after committing himself to mastering the Force; even so, it continued to be a mystery to him.

The Jedi Christian seeks to know not just the Force but also the Force above all forces, the Lord of the Force. The Lord of the Force is beyond knowing, yet invites knowing; the Lord of the Force is wholly other but became flesh and dwelt among us; the Lord of the Force is a mystery, a riddle, a seven-sided Rubik's Cube.

Today there are those who speak with great certitude from the oak-paneled confines of their comprehensive systematic theologies. To listen to them, one would conclude there are no questions about God, only answers, and mystery is something that appears only in fiction.

There are those who speak provincially, possessively, exclusively, competitively about God; our God is better than your God. Their god is made in their fallen, insecure image. Do not join them; run from them.

The way to God is the way of the mystics. Here all religions find some common ground, for our search for God begins and ends with our profession of incapacity and ignorance.

In the 1300s, an unidentified Christian sage described the early stages of the aspiring Christian's search for the Lord of the Force: "When you first begin, you find only darkness, and as it were a cloud of unknowing."

Enter this cloud of unknowing, because to remain outside it condemns you to a passionless, powerless, moribund life. To enter, though, is to leave behind the certainty, pride, and arrogance of those whose god is too small, whose god is trivialized, boxed in, and then used as a bludgeon against all challengers.

On occasion the shroud of clouds is thinned and we get glimpses of the One who cannot be known; though we, like the Apostle Paul, still see through a glass dimly, our vision is enhanced by our encounters with the divine. The Lord of the Force appeared in a burning bush, in a son called Jesus, in the written word, and in other ways, each an extraordinary revelation, but always confined and restricted to languages and symbols we can comprehend, so that our minds can grasp truth about aspects of God's being.

The Jedi Christian values the complexity of engaging with the holy mystery that can never be solved on this earth but must continually be explored and embraced. As with the mystics of old, our pursuit of God expands our knowledge of the holy, but the complete truth will always exist apart from the constraints of human language and perception. Words are inadequate to describe the Lord of the Force, as demonstrated by Christian writer A.W. Tozer, whose marvelous list of God's attributes, such as Incomprehensible, Infinite, and Omniscient, points to but can never quantify the wonders of God.

The inability of language, no matter how theologically rich, to reveal God to us was made clear to my father when, as a young man, he asked Tozer the secret to growing in the knowledge and practice of the holy. My father expected a deeply intellectual and profound response, but Tozer's pastoral reply lacked any lofty theological pretense. "Son," he said, "read the Bible and pray and you'll grow like a weed."

The ways of the Lord of the Force are beyond intellectual comprehension; nevertheless the Jedi devotes all of life to understanding and mastering the ways of the Lord of the Force. Our experience of God is beyond the intellect; therefore it is the journey, the quest, the pursuit that builds us.

CHAPTER 10

Don't Miss
the Big Reveal

Lost a planet, Master Obi-Wan has.
How embarrassing.

—YODA (*STAR WARS: EPISODE II.
ATTACK OF THE CLONES*)

Long ago God spoke to our ancestors in many
and various ways by the prophets, but in these
last days he has spoken to us by a Son.

—HEBREWS 1:1–2

J edi Master Obi-Wan is searching for an assassin
from the planet Kamino, but the location doesn't
show up in the comprehensive galaxy maps
archived at the Jedi Academy. Madame Jocasta Nu,

55

a Jedi archivist, concludes that the planet doesn't exist. Obi-Wan insists he heard descriptions of this planet long ago from a reliable and trustworthy friend, and he surmises aloud that the archives are incomplete. Yoda mocks Obi-Wan: "Lost a planet, Master Obi-Wan has. How embarrassing. . . ."

Finally one of the "younglings," a child and prospective Jedi in training, suggests that Obi-Wan go just south of the Rishi Maze, in the quadrant where he believes the "invisible" planet is located, and then follow the pull of gravity to its center. Following this inductive process allows Obi-Wan to discover the "missing" planet few believed existed.

When REM's Michael Stipe wrote the lyrics for *I've Been High,* he surrounded himself with dozens of spiritual books and manuscripts, among them the Bible. The song hauntingly chronicles the possibility of seeking and not finding the elusive truth that is right in front of you, somehow missing what he calls "the big reveal." Although our pure intellectual knowledge of God is forever shrouded in the cloud of unknowing, significant revelations from scripture and our experience of Him allow devoted seekers to discover what cannot be grasped by the mind alone. Tragically, many people miss the biggest reveal of all: God's revelation of Himself to humans.

Among God's big reveals is the created natural order, which conveys a complexity, magnitude, scope, and intelligence of design that all point toward God as a Force deserving our worship and praise. Also, the Apostle Paul describes the law of God as "written in our hearts," a reference to human conscience as the internal, universally revealed moral law known to all humans and hinting at the existence of a moral force and personality who is the author of that law. Following the gravitational pull of nature and moral law alone are enough to pull the seeker irresistibly to God, but there is more. The Jedi possess archives of Jedi wisdom, and so do aspiring Christians, whose Holy Scriptures, inspired by the Lord of the Force, describe human rebellion and announce God's loving pursuit of His wayward children.

Christians, in the spirit of the Jedi, gain insight and understanding from another reveal, the most stunning of all, reported by the writer of Hebrews: "Long ago God spoke to our ancestors in many and various ways by the prophets, but in these last days he has spoken to us by a Son, whom he appointed heir of all things, through whom he also created the worlds. He is the reflection of God's glory and the exact imprint of God's very being, and he sustains all things by his powerful word." This Son, of course, is Jesus.

Today, virtually everyone who knows of Jesus describes him as a great moral teacher and prophet. It is true he lived an exemplary life, but he also claimed to die for our sins and promised to defeat death by his resurrection from the dead on the third day. His disciples report that just before they saw him ascend into heaven, he explicitly told them he would prepare a place for his followers and one day would return for them. To stop short of accepting Jesus' own claims is to miss the biggest reveal of all. As C. S. Lewis observes, Jesus made some stunning assertions, and we are left to choose only one of three options: "he is either a liar, or he is a lunatic, or he is who he claimed to be—the Lord and only Son of God." If he is the son of God, it changes everything; we can no longer passively admire his teaching but must actively obey him as Lord.

In following Jesus, the aspiring Christian places all her trust in the biggest reveal of all, in him who claimed to be the truth, the way to the Father, and giver of life abundant and eternal.

CHAPTER 11

Meditate

Concentrate. . . . Feel the Force flow.

—YODA (*STAR WARS: EPISODE V.*
THE EMPIRE STRIKES BACK)

I commune with my heart in the night;
I meditate and search my spirit.

—PSALM 77:6

arly in Luke's Jedi training he concentrates on
using his lightsaber to defend himself against
the "seeker," or remote—a spherical, antennae-
covered chrome robot that moves quickly, hovering
and darting both playfully and menacingly in front

of him. As Luke becomes more proficient, Ben urges him to try again, this time with a helmet covering his eyes, forcing Luke to let go of his conscious self and see with an inner vision. After experiencing some success, Luke is exhilarated: "You know, I did feel something. I could almost see the remote."

Christians too can often point to a similar occasion where their mystical connection with the Lord of the Force was so real they could feel it. Our brushes with the divine are precious, and they can be sustained and nurtured through meditation. This close communion with God involves the whole person, instructing the mind, moving the will, warming the heart. Meditation is like digging a well in search of a fresh underground vein of water, or sending a kite skyward in search of the unseen breeze.

The sensation of being refreshed by cool water or propelled by wind in our sails that we first experienced as Jedi Christians is renewable through meditation. We may meditate in solitude or in the quietness of a contemplative community, but either way silence is a prerequisite. Meditation requires intentionally clearing our thoughts of all the high-pressure distractions and obligations of our lives. To restore his soul, the shepherd and Psalmist David spent hours beside still waters and in green pastures, meditating on the scriptures. Today our electronic lives pulsate manically, fast-paced, with noisy janglings and rapid-fire images. One can hardly imagine a life more sharply contrasted to David's or less conducive to spiritual restoration. We are culturally gluttonous and spiritually anorexic, uncritically devouring immense portions of a soul-starving culture, and then we wonder why all is not well with our soul. In a frazzled world, quiet meditation is the remedy and a requirement for all Christians, not an advanced spiritual exercise to be practiced by the exceptional few.

Meditating on God's written revelation and on the writings of wise Christians who came before us is a good place to start. Our *lectio divina,* or spiritual reading, then leads to what is called *discursive meditation,* the practice of reflecting on what we have read and on remembrances of our own encounters with God. If, as C. S. Lewis said, reason is the organ of truth and imagination the organ of meaning, then the combination of reading and reflection awakens our mind, heart, and entire being for prayer. Prayer takes many forms, one of which is expression of a longing for a deeper, more satisfying connection with God. Fasting, or going without food for a specified period of time, can also be a useful aid to focus on the spiritual over the physical, because each hunger pang becomes a reminder of the spiritual enterprise to which you are dedicated.

Reading, reflection, and prayer prepare our hearts for *contemplation,* which is defined by a former Trappist monk, James Finley, as "mystical union with God, a state of realized oneness with God, in which we rest in God and God rests in us, in which we are at home with God at home in us." Meditation is a prerequisite, setting the stage for the contemplative state. Like the Jedi knight who experienced the Force only when calm, the Christian's deepest meditation requires a physical and mental posture of stillness and alertness; still, when mystical oneness is achieved it is not evidenced in a feeling but in a state of awareness. In this moment of deep connection with the divine, we are fully aware that the spiritual is the core of reality and the physical is a temporary state. This is what the Christian mystic and poet William Blake meant when he observed that "if the doors of perception were cleansed, everything would appear to man as it is, infinite."

Meditation leading to contemplation is a rarity in much of today's Christian practice, especially in the evangelical and fundamentalist communities. This is odd, because Jesus set the example of daily meditation, often starting his day with prayer and praying in the evening too, as in the Garden of Gethsemane. The prayer he taught his disciples reveals his desire to consciously enter into God's presence and invite God into his each day. In this way he sought a life on earth as it is in heaven, harmonizing his personal will with that of God and His kingdom. Jesus' experience of oneness with God, which we have described as a contemplative state, was something he wanted all his disciples to experience. He prayed that Christians might enjoy this awareness of God, saying that "the glory that you have given me I have given them, so that they may be one, as we are one, I in them and you in me, that they may be completely one. . . ."

Even in this scientific age, people hunger for a deeper connection with God found through meditation. As Albert Einstein once commented, "The most beautiful and profound emotion we can experience is the sensation of the mystical. It is the course of all true science. . . . To know that what is impenetrable to us really exists . . . this knowledge, this feeling, is the center of true religion." Today some aspiring Jedi, so to speak, believe they must pursue other religions, especially Eastern traditions, to experience the contemplative life. Thomas Merton discovered this is not so. Having explored the contemplative wisdom of non-Christian mystics, shortly before his death he wrote a letter from Buddhist Thailand and reported that in going to Asia he learned that everything he was seeking had been present in his own Christian tradition all along.

Aspiring Jedi Christian, ours is a heritage rich with contemplatives whose meditation enriched their communion with God. Go and do likewise.

CHAPTER 12

Go Deep in a Shallow Age

Already know you that which you need.

—YODA, TO LUKE (*STAR WARS:*
EPISODE VI. RETURN OF THE JEDI)

These are the ones sown on rocky ground: when they
hear the word, they immediately receive it with joy.
But they have no root, and endure only for a while.

—MARK 4:16–17

O urs is a superficial age, a culture defined
by diversionary entertainment, mindless
amusements, and characterless celebrity.
There is no ballast for our souls in culture, and often

not even in faith, where religion itself sometimes mirrors the values and shallowness of this fallen world. This is Christianity Lite: no self-denial, no taking up a cross, no following Jesus on the contrarian path. Here the masses dance to the piper's tune, not to the symphony of the Lord of the Force. Lemminglike they march in lock step, claiming to be enlightened individualists, when they are dullards and conformists to the core. The art produced by our culture and faith are a monument to our poverty of spirit, betraying us in its soullessness, lifelessness; it is not divine in origin or aim. If we continue on this path, we are doomed.

Many who call themselves seekers are in truth dabblers, simply wading ankle-deep and playing on the shore of a vast, limitless ocean. We stay close by the beach, building sand castles, afraid to risk entering the fathomless waters where dwell the risks and rewards of the open sea. We wonder why we cannot catch an exhilarating spiritual wave like a surfer, or acquire a sailor's speed, with anchor up and sails at full mast, billowing with wind. The pleasures of the ocean are available only to those who go deeper and farther.

Behold, I remind you of a better way, lodged securely in our collective consciousness, for Master Yoda has said, "Already know you that which you need." Go deep in a shallow age; go deeper in faith, and you will be a force to enrich and bring gravitas to this hapless, fallen culture.

King David laid out a plan for deep faith in Psalm 1. He reminds us that going deeper requires non-conformity to the superficialities of culture: "Happy are those who do not follow the advice of the wicked or take the path of sinners or sit in the seat of scoffers."

Going deep requires concentrating on the sub-stance below the surface, building a solid foundation, sinking down roots in God and God's ways: "Their delight is in the law of the Lord and on his law they meditate day and night."

The Christian of this Jedi sort is solid, single-minded, stable, unmoved by trends in faith and culture; because of our depth we enjoy true wealth, and our life is rich in wholeness of spirit and steadfast rela-tionships with God and humans. "They are like a tree planted by streams of water, which yields fruit in its season, and their leaves do not wither. In all they do, they prosper." The Christian's substantial life points the world to a better way. The Jedi among us are eager to display an alternative to shallow living, because we know our superficial age and shallow faith will one day be revealed, judged, and destroyed. "The wicked are not so, but are like chaff that the wind drives away. Therefore the wicked will not stand in the judgment, nor sinners in the congregation of the righteous, for the Lord watches over the way of the righteous, but the way of the wicked will perish."

Deep faith enriches culture by creating beautiful, original art, crafted with care by today's counterparts to the builders of the original Hebrew Temple in Jerusalem, Bezalel and Oholiab, who are described as "filled with divine spirit, endowed with ability, intelligence, knowledge and skill in their craft." Deep faith enriches culture when Christians serve as ambassadors for the Lord of the Force: bilingual, fluent in both faith and culture, announcing God's intention to "make all things new." Deep faith enriches culture when, like resident aliens from the kingdom of God, we showcase authentic whole lives in contrast to the inauthentic, incomplete lives produced by our fallen culture.

Aspiring Jedi, I am warning you: remain in the superficial and your soul will be hungry, your breathing shallow, and your very life anemic. Go deeper! Fill your soul with the presence of the Lord of the Force, breathe rich spiritual oxygen, and feast on the nutrients of the living word, until the Lord of the Force is an all-consuming presence in your ever-deepening life.

CHAPTER 13

Aim High and Let Grace Fill the Gap

You want the impossible.
—LUKE, TO YODA (*STAR WARS:
EPISODE V. THE EMPIRE STRIKES BACK*)

Be perfect as your heavenly Father is perfect.
—JESUS (MATTHEW 5:48)

I was the best high jumper at Nicholas Junior High until Karden Kelly came to town and beat my best jump by almost a full foot. This athletic humiliation and personal epiphany made me rethink my achievements, and I began to question whether I should continue jumping at all.

The same thing happened to Luke Skywalker as he became overwhelmed with Yoda's high standards during his Jedi training. Yoda wanted him to levitate an aircraft out of the swamp, but Luke thought this was an impossible task—until he saw the diminutive Yoda lift it out with ease.

The single-minded follower of Jesus has also been given a seemingly impossible task: Jesus commanded his disciples to be perfect (a standard more foreboding than Karden Kelly's—or even Yoda's).

As with all the words spoken by Jesus, these must be understood in their fuller context. His exact words were delivered in his famous Sermon on the Mount: "You therefore must be perfect, as your heavenly Father is perfect." In this part of the sermon, Jesus is redefining the commandments in a way, making it clear that if we overlook the *spirit* of the law, we've as good as broken it ("If you lust after a woman you've committed adultery in your heart"; "If you hate your brother you have committed murder"). By radically restating the commandments, Jesus accomplishes two things. First, he sets a higher standard, providing us with our spiritual "Karden Kelly moment." Here we thought we were pretty decent law abiding people, and now we find out the bar is a full foot higher than we are currently jumping. Second, Jesus lays the foundation for his teaching about God's radical grace and love. He announces that the son of God has the authority to forgive sins, and in God's mercy and love our sins (now so apparent, given these higher standards) are bountifully forgiven!

Though Jedi-like we Christians are humbled daily by our lapses and failures, we remain courageous in our quest for perfection because we have learned to aim high and allow God to fill the gaps. By way of encouragement, C. S. Lewis observed, "Only those who try to resist temptation know how strong it is. . . . That is why bad people know very little about badness. They have lived a sheltered life by always giving in. We never find out the strength of the evil impulse inside us until we try to fight it: and Christ, because He was the only man who never yielded to temptation, is also the only man who knows to the full what temptation means—the only complete realist."

Aspiring Jedi, if you are aware of your failings it is probably because you are aiming high. To resolve the dissonance, don't lower your standards; just allow grace to carry you when you inevitably stumble. Grace is God's unmerited, undeserved favor; it is His gift of love, acceptance, and forgiveness to those who fall short in attempting perfection. In his recent song titled "Grace," Bono of U2 reminds us of grace's capacity to take our blame, cover our shame, remove our stains, and see and make even ugly things beautiful. Because of grace we are not humbled without relief; grace makes everything beautiful, even our botched attempts.

And so, aspiring Jedi Christian, continue to grow in love, reaching for the grace God offers, and extending that grace to other people on your journey. God your Father demands that you aim high, but He loves you with a perfect grace and restores beauty to your life, despite your failures.

CHAPTER 14

Trust the Lord of the Force

Concentrate on the moment.
Feel, don't think. Use your instincts.
—JEDI MASTER QUI-GON JINN,
TO ANAKIN SKYWALKER (*STAR WARS:
EPISODE I. THE PHANTOM MENACE*)

Trust in the Lord . . . and he shall direct your paths.
—PROVERBS 3:5–6, NEW KING JAMES VERSION

Each of us is most creative and productive when we are "in the flow," according to the findings of Mihaly Csikszentmihalyi, a researcher of motivation and creativity at the University of Chicago. His research reveals an almost mystical, energy-releasing synergy that occurs when an individual's one-of-a-kind personality, temperament, and skills are calibrated to specific tasks and situations calling for their unique abilities. Like white water in rapids, flow is a pure, freeing rush enabling us to reach peak performance in life.

The Jedi found themselves in the flow when they concentrated on trusting their feelings and instincts instead of depending strictly on logic. We Christians find the flow through ignoring the demands of our will and wholeheartedly sensing and trusting the will of the Lord of the Force. King Solomon, considered one of the wisest men who ever lived, advised, "Trust in the Lord with all your heart, and do not rely on your own insight. In all your ways acknowledge him, and he will give you the desires of your heart," or as another translation says, "He will direct your paths."

Christians devoted to the Jedi path are trained to accept a counterintuitive teaching: Lose your life and you'll find it, and the first will be last and the last first. Humanly, our first instinct is to think we will attain our greatest satisfaction when we get what we want, so we concentrate our time and energy on fulfilling our desires. Yet the old adage warns us to be careful what we wish for, because we just might get it. Centuries of human experience reveal the hollowness of achieving our goals if they are the wrong ones.

Solomon learned to know and trust the Lord of the Force, to acknowledge Him in all of life, which meant that he harmonized his will with the Lord's will and ultimately received the desires of his heart because God's will became his desire. As a young man about to take the throne, Solomon prayed, "I am only a little child; give your servant an understanding mind to govern your people, able to discern between good and evil." God appeared in a dream that night, telling Solomon that because he asked for wisdom instead of riches for himself he would receive a wise and discerning mind *and* would also receive what he didn't ask for, riches and honor. To this day, we refer to "the wisdom of Solomon"; his wealth surpassed that of his contemporaries. Amazing things happen in the flow!

Our minds can grasp God's will in a general sense—don't kill, don't commit adultery, don't lie or steal—but we yearn to find God in the specific decisions of life. What kind of work should I do? Who should I marry? How should I respond to this distressing family situation? Jesus mastered living in an energizing, confident flow with God each day, and we can too. He arose well before dawn to spend time with God, acknowledging that he willed one thing: to do the will of the Father. He brought that sense of God's continuous presence into all his interactions.

Jesus displayed the authority characteristic of flow by his decisiveness in every situation. Once, even though the disciples pointed to people waiting for healing, he intuitively knew it was time to go to the next village. This sounds strange; why not stay and meet the needs right there? Jesus sensed his work was finished there and followed God's leading to meet more pressing needs in another village. Another time, when the disciples brought a paralyzed man for healing, instead of immediately relieving the man of his paralysis Jesus looked to a much deeper need and said, "Your sins are forgiven." His sense of God's direction in his life was so constant that he was able to intuitively synchronize his decisions in every aspect of his daily life.

Jesus' spiritual instincts were perfectly calibrated with God's will, so he trusted them. Qui-Gon says that the aspiring Jedi Anakin "can see things before they happen." The more intimately the Christian knows the Lord of the Force, the more she will be able to trust that her instincts are harmonized with God's will.

Aspiring Jedi Christian, there is nothing more exciting than starting the day with a sense that God's presence can flow through you if you'll flow with the stream of His will. Use your mind, master God's Word, and seek the counsel of other wise Christians; but your minute-by-minute source of guidance is the flow of the Spirit, who enlightens us, as we trust the Lord of the Force. When we bring our heart's desire into harmony with His will, He will direct our path.

CHAPTER 15

know and Love the Word

Remember, Obi-Wan. If the prophecy is true,
your apprentice is the only one
who can bring the Force back into balance.

—MACE WINDU, TO OBI-WAN (*STAR WARS:
EPISODE I. THE PHANTOM MENACE*)

Oh, how I love Your law!
It is my meditation all the day.

—PSALM 119:97

A spiring Jedi are sent to the Academy to master the ancient laws, which hold the secrets
of the Force, providing the Jedi with purpose,

79

power, and tranquility. Christian disciples find purpose, power, and tranquillity by learning the ancient words recorded in our Holy Book, the repository of the spiritual ways governing the universe that lead us to know and love the Lord of the Force.

This Holy Book, the Bible, is the best-selling book of all time. Depending on the translation, there are approximately 785,000 words in it, divided into 31,101 numbered verses. There are about 8,000 predictions, 6,468 commands, 1,260 promises, and 3,294 questions. The sixty-six books of the Bible include poetry, wisdom literature, history, parables, prophecies, apocalyptic (end times) writing, laws, and memoirlike letters. In addition to its great variety, what is it about this book that has drawn people of all ages and every nationality to its pages for thousands of years?

King David's reasons for loving this book are seen in these excerpts from one of his most expressive psalms:

> Happy are those whose way is blameless, who
>   walk in the law of the Lord. . . .
> How can young people keep their way pure? By
>   guarding it according to your word. . . .
> The law of your mouth is better to me than thousands of gold and silver pieces. . . .

I know, O Lord, that your judgments are right,
and that in faithfulness you have humbled
me. . . .
Your commandment makes me wiser than my
enemies, for it is always with me. . . .
I have more understanding than all my teachers,
for your decrees are my meditation. I understand more than the aged, for I keep your
precepts. . . .
Your word is a lamp to my feet and a light to my
path. Your word is like milk for the newborn
baby and meat for the growing child. . . .

Others cherish this book because it is the greatest love
story ever told, the story of God's love for us. It reveals
truth, offers words of eternal life, and is the tool God
uses like a gardener to prune our spiritual lives. Some
will quote the words of Paul, mentor to Timothy: "But
as for you, continue in what you have learned and
firmly believed, knowing from whom you learned it,
and how from childhood you have known the sacred
writings that are able to instruct you for salvation
through faith in Christ Jesus. All scripture is inspired
by God and is useful for teaching, for reproof, for correction, and for training in righteousness, so that

everyone who belongs to God may be proficient, equipped for every good work."

Though the Word serves a practical purpose as a much-needed resource for spiritual nurture and guidance, and though it can and should be studied and wrestled with intellectually, I advise aspiring Jedi to know and love the book in a more intimate way, as you would a person with whom you have a deep relationship. Think of the Word as a friend with whom you spend considerable time and whom you grow to love more each day, with an intensity matching the ardor of Elizabeth Barrett Browning's classic poem:

How do I love thee? Let me count the ways.
I love thee to the depth and breadth and height
My soul can reach, when feeling out of sight
For the ends of Being and ideal Grace.
I love thee to the level of every day's
Most quiet need, by sun and candle-light.
I love thee freely, as men strive for Right;
I love thee purely, as they turn from Praise.
I love thee with a passion put to use
In my old griefs, and with my childhood's faith.
I love thee with a love I seemed to lose
With my lost saints,—I love thee with the breath,

Smiles, tears, of all my life!—and, if God choose,
I shall but love thee better after death.

You may never have seen this kind of intimate knowledge and love for the Word; in my life it has been both an inescapable reality and an invaluable gift. It is the reason I still spend time with the Bible every day, even when I am at my busiest. I cannot explain exactly when and how I came to this understanding, but I can describe it.

When I was four years old my father took me to his favorite clearing in the woods. He promised if I was very quiet I might see a deer, and despite my clamorous presence a deer appeared. More memorable than the animal is the image of my father's silhouette with an open Bible on his lap. Though just a boy, I intuitively sensed that he experienced God's presence in that clearing and in that book. It was the first of many times I observed my father's lifelong companionship with this book.

Years later, as a teen, I listened as my grandfather read aloud from the Bible in a stand of towering redwood trees. From the age of fifteen until her death at age ninety-three, my grandmother read through the Bible at least once each year. I remember them sitting quietly and reverentially in a favorite chair, with the Bible open in front of them, gazing off as they ponder these words that seem new and fresh each day.

Last weekend, I watched my grandson Eli, my son's son, fold his hands and pray over a meal. I've witnessed five generations of Staubs find their way to God and discovered the mysterious ways of the spiritual universe through this book passed from one generation to the next.

This is a knowing, loving relationship that will last a lifetime. My father, now in his eighties, lives in a small apartment a building away from my mother, who suffers from Alzheimer's and from whom he was inseparable for more than fifty years. Dad's best friend in the retirement community just died of cancer, and my brother, brain damaged from birth, lives in a nursing home two hundred miles away from my father; Dad misses all three of them and many other people he no longer sees. Dad lived life well and could justifiably sink into despondency, bitterness, or disbelief due to his circumstances. But instead, every Tuesday he leads a Bible study packed with older people like him, who love the Word and gather to find happiness, light for their path, and food for their souls. Right now, he is studying Paul's epistle to the Philippians, where he reads, "I can do all things through Christ who strengthens me."

How I love the Word, oh Lord, and how I yearn to see aspiring Christians know and love it as generations have before. For centuries, God has mysteriously revealed Himself through this book, and He will do the same in your life if you move beyond the words on the page to the living Word. Allow Him to author your life story through the living authority of His Word. There is no higher calling or sustaining power for the aspiring Jedi than day and night to know, love, and meditate on God as revealed through His Word.

CHAPTER 16

obey the Word

Partially. But it also obeys your commands.

—OBI-WAN, WHEN LUKE ASKS WHETHER
THE FORCE CONTROLS HIS ACTIONS
(*STAR WARS: EPISODE IV. A NEW HOPE*)

Blessed rather are those who hear
the word of God and obey it!

—JESUS, TO HIS DISCIPLES (LUKE 11:28)

When Luke Skywalker challenges his father's loyalty to the dark side, Darth Vader replies, "You don't know the power of the dark side. I must obey my master."

Vader's allegiance to the dark side is complete; he is pledged to obey it.

Christians aspiring to the Jedi ways know that the Word is to be known and loved, but it is also to be obeyed. Unlike Vader's authority, God is unquestionably deserving of our obedience. The willingness to submit to the will of another has fallen out of favor, however. We react negatively to the very implication of following instructions, behaving in accordance with a law, or submitting to someone else's control—even God's! The seeds of this rebellion were sown in Eden; they experienced a modern resurgence in the 1960s when everybody was urged to resist authority—back then we were told not to trust anyone over the age of thirty!

My generation's skepticism toward authority was not without justification. The Vietnam War and Watergate created widespread distrust of the government. The feminist movement exposed the abuses of male domination. The civil rights movement raised questions about religious fundamentalists justifying discrimination against blacks. The "Leave It to Beaver," everything-is-OK family image was exposed as hypocritical in homes where everything wasn't OK beneath the façade.

In a classic case of throwing the baby out with the bath water, my generation threw out respect for any and *all* authority, and the result was a libertine free-for-all of drug abuse, unrestricted sexual debauchery, and the jettisoning of any traditional mores. The times were changing, and individual, relativistic morality was at the heart of the changes. Ongoing, systematic perpetuation of this approach was assured once situational ethics became part of official policy in public school education, teaching that right and wrong depends on the situation, and that each individual alone discerns the right choice through a process of "values clarification." Where once ethical decisions were based on a common moral code largely shaped by religious teaching, these decisions were now viewed as situational and up to the individual to decide. Born and raised in this system, even many Christians aspiring to Jedi wisdom have been taught to place confidence in their autonomous moral authority, but they are sometimes unaware of the devastating personal, cultural, and spiritual consequences of this approach.

Culturally, the result of our moral lawlessness is well documented, as psychologist David Myers observes:

> We are better paid, better fed, better housed, better educated and healthier than ever before . . . yet for 30 years America slid into a deepening social

recession. . . . The divorce rate has doubled, the teen suicide has tripled, the recorded violent crime rate has quadrupled, the prison population has quintupled, the percentage of babies born to unmarried parents has sextupled, cohabitation (a predictor of future divorce) has increased sevenfold and depression has soared to ten times the pre-World War II level, by one estimate.

We have learned a lesson spiritually as well. Just a decade after Bob Dylan observed that the times are a-changin', he penned lyrics describing what he learned from the sixties, concluding that everybody serves somebody and ultimately it will either be the devil or the Lord. Our choice is not *whether* we will obey someone; we only get to choose *whom* we will obey, and the fallout of the sixties makes it pretty clear who most people are serving.

As Jedi devotees, we Christians pledge to seek and do God's will, to obey the Lord of the Force, who in his Holy Book has revealed laws that are clear and not open to debate. This is what Mark Twain meant when he quipped, "It's not what I *don't* understand in the Bible that bothers me; it is what I *do* understand!" An example would be the Ten Commandments, which are considered passé by many people today, though they are not at all onerous and as a matter of fact describe patterns of behavior designed by our Maker to produce our personal fulfillment and joy. They still govern the Jedi Christian's moral choices and behavior:

1. You shall have no other Gods before me.
2. You shall not make for yourselves an idol.
3. You shall not misuse the name of the LORD your God.
4. Remember the Sabbath day by keeping it holy.
5. Honor your father and your mother.
6. You shall not murder.
7. You shall not commit adultery.
8. You shall not steal.
9. You shall not give false testimony.
10. You shall not covet.

A few thousand years later, Jesus reaffirmed these ten commands, summarizing them by saying: "You shall love the Lord your God with all your heart, and with all your soul, and with all your mind. This is the greatest and first commandment. And a second is like it: You shall love your neighbor as yourself." He further simplified the law into a "golden rule," to "do unto others as you would have them do unto you." Finally, Jesus told his disciples, "A new commandment I give you, that you love one another."

Each of Jesus' restatements of the Ten Commandments puts an emphasis on our love for God and each
other. Jesus emphasized love because although the law
points the way to God's will and can serve as a societal
restraint against evil, the law also reveals our need
for God's grace and love, since at times we fail to
meet God's standard. Second, Jesus emphasized love,
because for all the benefits the law offers, only the person who loves God wants to do His will and obey His
laws anyway!

God's laws can never abolish wickedness in a society without love for God or a desire to obey Him.
Unfortunately, the combination of Jesus' emphasis on
love and the 1960s emphasis on freedom from authority has resulted in a distortion of Jesus' teaching. Today
many people mistakenly rationalize their disobedience
of God's commandments under the guise of "doing the
loving thing." A person's unfaithfulness to a spouse is
excused by believing the new relationship makes the
person happy, and by a conviction that since God loves
us and wants us to be happy, this must be OK.

In Edward Albee's recent and radical turn-of-the-
century play *The Goat,* the key character, Martin, a
successful architect, is having sex with a goat, but he
wants his wife not to worry because he still loves her;
he has never been unfaithful to her (with a human);

and though people *think* what he is doing is wrong, they should just accept him and *love* him the way he is. Albee states the postmodern dilemma in the extreme to make a point: the human ability to rationalize can make any act seem like the loving—and therefore the right—thing.

Jesus anticipated this problem and said he did not come to destroy the law, but to fulfill it. In other words, the law of love does not replace the requirement that we obey God's revealed law. As a matter of fact, the law stands as the most reliable guide to help us properly define what the loving thing is.

Jesus also taught that there are consequences for disobeying God's law. The Jedi Christian understands that individuals who knowingly and perpetually disobey God's law cannot expect God's blessing; conversely, obeying God brings His blessing. "See, I have set before you today life and prosperity, death and adversity. If you obey the commandments of the Lord your God . . . the Lord your God will bless you in the land that you are entering to possess. But if your heart turns away and you do not hear, but are led astray to bow down to other gods and serve them, I declare to you today that you shall perish."

For many aspiring Christians, disobedience is all that stands between them and the free and full experience of God's blessings. My advice is that you turn from those areas of disobedience by replacing them with the habits of obedience. Turn away from the things God hates by embracing the attitudes and behaviors God loves. You will learn that, like every habit, the more you cultivate obedience the easier it becomes. This was observed by Teresa of Avila, who once said, "I know the power obedience has of making things easy which seem impossible."

Our obedience is not required only in the big and dramatic areas of life, but in each moment of each day. William Barclay trumpeted the virtue of daily obedience: "The greatest thing is a life of obedience in the routine things of everyday life. No amount of fine feeling can take the place of faithful doing."

Faithful choices and daily obedience in matters large and small: this is the way of the Jedi for every Christian.

CHAPTER 17

Believe to See

Sometimes, when you believe
something to be real, it becomes real.
—ANAKIN SKYWALKER (*STAR WARS:
EPISODE II. ATTACK OF THE CLONES*)

Without faith it is impossible to please God.
—HEBREWS 11:6

It is a universal spiritual truth that you must first believe in order to see. As if speaking in a riddle, Obi-Wan tells Luke, "Your eyes can deceive you. Don't trust them. Stretch out with your feelings."

The Christian seeking Jedi wisdom understands that faith is more than a feeling; it is "the assurance of things hoped for, the conviction of things not seen." Faith is a foundation of our heritage as Christians; "indeed, by faith our ancestors received approval."

You come from a long line of heroic saints whose stories reveal the nature of faith. Noah was warned of a coming flood and told to build a boat while the weather was clear; Abraham was told to set out for a land he would inherit without being told in advance where he was going; the ineloquent and armyless Moses was sent to deliver a speech to the mighty Pharaoh demanding that he release the Hebrews; David was sent before the heavily armed Goliath with nothing but a slingshot and five stones. Through faith, our spiritual ancestors "conquered kingdoms, administered justice, obtained promises, shut the mouths of lions, quenched raging fire, escaped the edge of the sword, won strength out of weakness, became mighty in war, put foreign armies to flight."

Faith is essential to the spiritual dimension. Your spiritual experience cannot exceed the boundaries of your faith; therefore lack of faith is the greatest impediment to experiencing God in daily life. But do we resolve doubts with faith, or with a silent, nagging agnosticism? When we sense God leading us out of our comfort zone, do we obey? When have we truly relied on God for daily bread? If God called on us to do so, which of us would build a boat in clear weather, or set out on a journey without knowing the destination?

Yet without a life of faith it is impossible to please God. As spiritual writer Kathleen Norris observes, faith resides at the intersection of "belief, doubt, and sacred ambiguity."

We need faith to believe. A recent cartoon pictured a lovely couple leaving the cathedral and commenting to the pastor, "Good sermon, Reverend, but all that God stuff was pretty far-fetched." As an aspiring Jedi, you are dedicating your life to someone you have never seen and building it on an infrastructure of beliefs about things unseen; without faith this might seem far-fetched. We humans are afraid to act on what we cannot see, yet belief is the prerequisite for sight. As Augustine says, "Faith is to believe what you do not see; the reward of this faith is to see what you believe." This is not to say faith makes us delusional. What we see by faith exists; we just can't see it without faith. The spiritual laws of the universe dictate that our faith activates our spiritual insight. Faith is the light shined into an unmarked, darkened cave that, once illuminated, reveals sparkling diamonds waiting to be mined.

We need faith in times of doubt. Faith always requires stepping into the unknown; its very nature straddles the fence dividing possible from impossible, known from unknown, doubt from certainty. Imagine the derision heaped on Noah by his neighbors. Did Noah have second thoughts as he built the Ark on a blue-sky day? As Abraham secured his son Isaac on a mound of sticks and lifted a knife high overhead, did he not question God—or his own sanity—looking into the frightened eyes of a boy facing doom at the hands of what appeared to be a hopelessly deranged father?

Blaise Pascal, the master of probability, resolves the conundrum this way: "In faith there is enough light for those who want to believe and enough shadows to blind those who don't." A young boy suffered convulsions since birth; his desperate father brought him to Jesus and said, "If you are able to do anything, have pity on us and help us." Jesus said to him, "If you are able!—All things can be done for the one who believes." The father immediately blurted out, "I believe; help my unbelief!" Though clouded by shadows of doubt, there was enough light for belief, and Jesus healed the son.

We need faith in times of sacred ambiguity. Ask the learned champion of reason Thomas Aquinas how to unlock the imponderable mysteries of belief and you will hear him say, "To one who has faith, no explanation is necessary. To one without faith, no explanation is possible." What may sound like a flip comment is actually words of wisdom from a seasoned veteran of faith. When my brother was born with brain damage, my family faced the age-old question of how God can be both all-powerful and all-loving and still allow something like this to happen. The novelist Norman Mailer told me he wrestled with the same issue as he thought about the Holocaust.

I can reach a level of understanding about this paradox by placing it in the context of human failure (in my brother's case, a doctor's error was involved), or in the context of human free will and fallenness (the Holocaust being a demonstrable manifestation of human wickedness). However, my best efforts still leave imponderables, which I choose to resolve by placing faith in the all-loving, all-powerful God. Mailer solves the dilemma by concluding that God is all-loving, but not all-powerful. For him, no explanation is possible without eliminating the belief in an all-powerful God. Because I've resolved the question by placing my trust in an all-powerful and all-loving God, in my case, an explanation is no longer necessary.

So, aspiring Jedi, each of us builds a life of faith on a foundation infested with unbelief, doubt, and sacred ambiguity, yet in our fervent desire to know and please God we pray the sincere prayer of the father who sought healing for his son: "I believe; help my unbelief."

CHAPTER 18

The Lord of the Force You Are Not

I should be! Someday I will be.

—ANAKIN, TO PADMÉ, AFTER SHE REMINDS
HIM THAT HE IS NOT ALL-POWERFUL
(*STAR WARS: EPISODE II. ATTACK OF THE CLONES*)

Your will be done, on earth as it is in heaven.

—JESUS, TEACHING THE DISCIPLES
TO PRAY (MATTHEW 6:10)

Why did Darth Vader leave the Jedi to serve the dark side?

As a young boy, Anakin Skywalker exposes his anger and frustration in a conversation with Senator Padmé when finally she tells him there are some things nobody can fix, reminding him that he is not all-powerful. His chilling response reveals his vulnerability to the dark side even as a young man, "I should be! Someday I will be. I will be the most powerful Jedi ever! I promise you, I will even learn to stop people from dying."

Anakin becomes Darth Vader because he lusts for power. The Jedi knew they could *use* the Force, the energy that binds the galaxies, but to aspire to *match* the unlimited power of the Force was out of the question. No matter how powerful the Jedi were, they knew they could not be omnipotent. So it is with the Christian whose training begins by recognizing limitations—namely, there is a Lord of the Force and you are not it! You will never truly know the Lord of the Force whom you seek until you master this important truth.

That the Lord of the Force exists is one thing; for humans to acknowledge and pay Him His proper due is another. Interestingly, a most compelling argument for the existence of God is the irrepressible human desire to worship, as Ralph Waldo Emerson observes: "A person will worship something, have no doubt about that." In a strange turn of events, from the very beginning with Adam and Eve, human worship has been diverted away from God and to virtually anything and everything else.

A good way to test the object of your worship is to evaluate who or what you think about most; your private thoughts reveal your innermost love. Emerson believed that what you love in private is likely to become public: "We may think our tribute is paid in secret in the dark recesses of our hearts, but it will out. That which dominates our imaginations and our thoughts will determine our lives, and our character."

By the time the Ten Commandments were delivered, humans had given themselves over to pursuit and glorification of their own private loves, displacing God with idols of their own making. In the very moment Moses was receiving the commandments, the idolatrous children of Israel were forging a golden calf. Behind each pretender to God's throne lurks the power-hungry human ego, growing like a cancer, willful and defiant and unwilling to bow to any authority but its own. Nobel laureate Aleksandr Solzhenitsyn poignantly describes the obsession the human ego has with itself: "The Universe has as many different centers as there are living beings in it."

What are the consequences of placing ourselves at the center of the universe, a place reserved exclusively for God? Without the sun's centering gravitational pull, the planets would spin out of control, wild, reckless, directionless, hurtling toward certain disintegration and doom. So too our human saga is documented in the wild gyrations of our foolish behavior. Adam and Eve's declaration of independence from God brought marital stress; their son Cain murdered his brother Abel; and within a few generations, we are told, the inclination of human hearts was "only evil continually." When God is displaced, His wonderful gifts become distorted and made grotesque: sex degenerates into pornography, excessive eating produces obesity, art becomes only self-expression instead of an act of worship, money becomes an end instead of a means of providing for our needs. Each abuse occurs as we set aside some aspect of our life and call it our own to manage in our way on our terms.

Yet as the Calvinist theologian and statesman Abraham Kuyper famously said, "There is not one square inch on earth over which God does not declare, 'this is mine.'" God's comprehensive claim over all the earth, of course, includes you, your will, and every aspect of your life. The Christian's progress toward maturity begins by embracing and obeying the commandment that "you shall have no other gods before me."

For the Jedi in the making, each day starts with the unshakable knowledge expressed in this simple prayer: "There is a Lord of the Force, and it is not I. My life is yours, oh Lord. May the words of my mouth and meditations of my heart in each moment of this day be acceptable in your sight." It is difficult to over-state the radical change evoked by wholeheartedly embracing this prayer. Virtually everything in our cul-ture sends the deceptive, alluring message that you are your life's highest priority, and that your sole purpose is to satisfy your own needs, desires, and will. Each day we arise and worship ourselves; we unquestioningly commit to "do it my way," "look out for number one," and "be all I can be," and everyone around us agrees that this is good!

This attitude even characterizes some churches, which are structured around meeting our felt needs. Like the local malls, their aim is to please us and every member of our family as consumers. As A. W. Tozer presciently observed: "Christianity today is man-centered, not God-centered. God is made to wait patiently, even respectfully, on the whims of men . . . to persuade these self-sufficient souls to respond to His generous offers. God will do almost anything, even using salesmanship methods and talking down to them in the chummiest way imaginable. This view of things is, of course, a kind of religious romanticism, which while it often uses flattering and sometimes embarrassing terms in praise of God, manages nevertheless to make man the star of the show."

When Jesus said the first requirement for becoming his disciple is to "deny yourself," he was emphasizing the simple fact that you cannot follow him and yourself at the same time. One force has got to be in control of your life's direction, affections, and activities. If it is Jesus, it cannot be you; and if it is you then there's no room for Jesus. Whether in the culture or the church, the Jedi turns from a self-serving life to one centered in God.

Emerson's final word on the subject is a cautionary one. "Therefore, it behooves us to be careful what we worship, for what we are worshipping we are becoming."

By daily seeking God's desires over yours, your accumulated actions and activities will become an homage to God, not to the self. Over a lifetime, this pursuit of holiness will lead you to become more like the Lord of the Force. The Christian seeking Jedi wisdom always acknowledges that *there is a Lord of the Force, and I am not it.* Only when you fully and deeply embrace this truth and order your daily life around it will you enter the arena for the spiritual war that is the destiny of every such Christian. Only those who accept their limitations and trust themselves to the limitless power of the Lord of the Force are prepared to face the dark side unafraid.

Part 4

FIGHTING

CHAPTER 19

Changed

To control your anger is to be a Jedi.
—ANAKIN, EXPLAINING TO PADMÉ
HOW A JEDI CHANGES (*STAR WARS:
EPISODE II. ATTACK OF THE CLONES*)

So if anyone is in Christ, there is a new
creation: everything old has passed away;
see, everything has become new!
2 CORINTHIANS 5:17

Yesterday a Jungian psychologist friend told me, "Who you are is pretty well set by the age of nine . . . people don't change. People *can't* change."

This, of course, is news to Jesus, who pretty much changes everybody he meets; he is a transforming presence. Unless you are a delusional psychotic out of touch with reality, or a nine-year-old who wants to keep playing marbles the rest of your life, the possibility of change is a positive thing—and there is a change coming.

At the cosmic level, we are hurtling through time and space toward a single moment when the trumpet of God will sound, we will all be changed from these physical bodies into spiritual ones, and God will craft a new heaven and new earth. At the personal level, a change as radical as the metamorphosis of a caterpillar to a butterfly is in store for every aspiring Christian in the authentic process of seeking, knowing, and submitting to the Lord of the Force. This is the exact image the Apostle Paul uses to describe the radical change Jesus brings to life: "I appeal to you therefore, brothers and sisters, by the mercies of God, to present your bodies as a living sacrifice, holy and acceptable to God, which is your spiritual worship. Do not be conformed to this world, but be transformed by the renewing of your minds, so that you may discern what is the will of God—what is good and acceptable and perfect. For by the grace given to me I say to everyone among you not to think of yourself more highly than you ought to think."

In these sayings, Paul tells us about the process and nature of our metamorphosis. It starts with yielding to God, which is described as an act of worship. Jesus laid down his life for us, and it is a reasonable response to voluntarily lay down our own life as an expression of thanks, putting us in the right frame of mind—humility—to understand God's will for our life. Where once we placed the greatest confidence in our way of thinking, we realize that God's ways are higher than our ways, and His thoughts are higher than our thoughts; we no longer think more highly of ourselves than we should. Just as yielding our will is based on a desire to be like Jesus, so too, humility of mind is inspired by Jesus:

> Do nothing from selfish ambition or conceit, but in humility regard others as better than yourselves. Let each of you look not to your own interests, but to the interests of others. Let the same mind be in you that was in Christ Jesus, who, though he was in the form of God, did not regard equality with God as something to be exploited, but emptied himself, taking the form of a slave, being born in human likeness. And being found in human form, he humbled

himself and became obedient to the point of death—
even death on a cross.

As your mind is renewed, everything changes.
You now will recognize the fallenness of the world and
no longer desire to be confirmed to it; rather, you are
transformed into a person who only wants to know
and do God's will. By choosing the word *metamorphosis* (translated *transformed* in the first quotation from
his letter to the Romans), Paul is saying that the person
who aspires to conform to the world is a like an earth-
bound, unattractive caterpillar; the person who pursues
God's will can fly like a beautiful, colorful butterfly.

As you undergo these changes, you will begin to
identify your God-given potential and to offer your
talents to serve God alongside other transformed people: "For as in one body we have many members, and
not all the members have the same function, so we,
who are many, are one body in Christ, and individually
we are members one of another. We have gifts that dif-
fer according to the grace given to us: prophecy, in
proportion to faith; ministry, in ministering; the
teacher, in teaching; the exhorter, in exhortation; the
giver, in generosity; the leader, in diligence; the com-
passionate, in cheerfulness."

Your transformation also affects your everyday attitudes and behavior:

> Let love be genuine; hate what is evil, hold fast to what is good; love one another with mutual affection; outdo one another in showing honor. Do not lag in zeal, be ardent in spirit, serve the Lord. Rejoice in hope, be patient in suffering, persevere in prayer. Contribute to the needs of the saints; extend hospitality to strangers. Bless those who persecute you; bless and do not curse them. Rejoice with those who rejoice, weep with those who weep. Live in harmony with one another; do not be haughty, but associate with the lowly; do not claim to be wiser than you are. Do not repay anyone evil for evil, but take thought for what is noble in the sight of all. If it is possible, so far as it depends on you, live peaceably with all.

The aspiring Jedi's complete transformation of will, mind, attitude, and behavior is what the Apostle Paul was referring to when he said, "if anyone is in Christ, there is a new creation: everything old has passed away; see, everything has become new!"

In *Star Wars: Episode IV. A New Hope* (the original film), Han Solo is transformed from a self-centered mercenary into a friend and ally to Luke Skywalker and Princess Leia. Luke is transformed from a reckless young guy ruled by passion into a Jedi who can control his emotions and effectively use the force. We resonate with stories where characters change for the good, because deep down each of us wants to be transformed into a better person. We want to believe that even if we make a mess of our life it is still possible one day to morph into the heroic ideal.

There is an interesting story about George Lucas's remake of the *Star Wars* (original film) final cut. In the original version there was a question about whether Han Solo or the bounty hunter Greedo shot first. Lucas edited the new DVD versions to make it clear that Greedo shot first because he did not want Han Solo to be perceived as a murderer. In an interview he said he didn't see how you could redeem someone who kills in cold blood. Lucas confirms the importance of Solo's transformation as a central theme of the story and also reveals a concern that some people may be beyond redemption.

A certain fatalism can creep into the worldview on display in *Star Wars,* which seeks the balance of light and darkness, rather than the eradication of darkness. Sometimes dualists (believing there is only dark and light and nothing over them) conclude that at their core people are either one or the other, dark or light. Apparently Lucas believes Han is essentially a child of the light who just needs his good side coaxed out of him, but had he murdered in cold blood it would indicate he was essentially from the dark side and could never cross into the light. In Eastern thought, this fatalism is called karma.

In the Bible (our Jedi Christian manual), we learn that every human can and must be changed and that such a change is possible for anyone. At the heart of your metamorphosis from spiritual caterpillar to butterfly is God's unmerited favor, called grace, which can make the ugliest thing beautiful. Grace flows from God, who is love, and is above, over, and beyond karma. This is why the Apostle Paul can say: "Who will separate us from the love of Christ? Will hardship, or distress, or persecution, or famine, or nakedness, or peril, or sword? No, in all these things we are more than conquerors through him who loved us. For I am convinced that neither death, nor life, nor angels, nor rulers, nor things present, nor things to come, nor powers, nor height, nor depth, nor anything else in all creation, will be able to separate us from the love of God in Christ Jesus our Lord."

So, aspiring Jedi, as a follower of Jesus enfolded in God's grace you are now prepared for the trials posed by the dark side. You are ready, because you've been changed; spiritually, you are no longer crawling like a caterpillar. You are flying.

CHAPTER 20

"Always Two There Are, a Master and an Apprentice"

Always two there are, a master and an apprentice.

—YODA, TO MACE WINDU
(*STAR WARS: EPISODE I. THE PHANTOM MENACE*)

When Jesus turned and saw them following, he said to them, "What are you looking for?" They said to him, "Rabbi" [which, translated, means "teacher"]. . . .

—JOHN 1:38

E very Jedi Knight was exceptionally strong in the Force, but to become a Jedi master, a Jedi needed to possess the patience to teach essential Jedi skills to Padawan, the younger, eager generations of would-be Jedi. The masters personally selected their understudies, who were usually young and always showed unusual promise in the Force. Obi-Wan and Yoda mentored Luke Skywalker, and once he was proficient in the Force, Luke graduated from student to teacher. He then searched the galaxy for other prospective Jedi, starting an Academy and training those strong in the Force. In this way, Jedi wisdom and skill was transferred from one generation to the next.

Likewise, the knowledge of the aspiring Christian is transferred from the master to an apprentice, who then becomes a master to the next generation. In Jesus' day, most young men would be thoroughly trained in the Torah, the Jewish holy books, and by the age of twelve they would present themselves to their teacher, the rabbi, for consideration to become disciples, official apprentices to that specific rabbi. The rabbi would determine whether or not the disciple showed sufficient promise to emulate the rabbi, and after selecting a few charges he would devote himself to their development into mature disciples, thoroughly equipped to become rabbis who could teach others.

Only the most devoted could enter into apprenticeship with Rabbi Jesus, because he made it clear that to be his disciple required self-denial and willingness to give up everything, even family and possessions, to take up a cross and follow him wherever he might lead. He apprenticed twelve disciples who learned by observing him, spending time with him, and listening to him. Learning the spiritual life has always been experiential and happens best outside the classroom. Moses instructed Jewish parents to recite the Shema Prayer: "Hear, O Israel: The Lord is our God, the Lord alone. You shall love the Lord your God with all your heart, and with all your soul, and with all your might. Keep these words that I am commanding you today in your heart." He then commanded them to teach them "to your children and talk about them when you are at home and when you are away, when you lie down and when you rise up." For a Jewish child, everyday life was a classroom!

The training of Jesus' disciples followed this pattern, with most lessons learned in a common situation or in conversation along the way to a destination. On occasion, the twelve were sent out on short assignments where they experienced modest success and exuberant failure, all of which created teachable moments.

Discipleship always requires "unlearning," which is why one of Jesus' most common expressions was, "You have heard it said . . ." followed shortly by "But I say to you. . . ." All we know prior to our training with the master is either obvious or wrong, which is why the process of apprenticeship takes time. Over three years, Jesus invested in his disciples, taught by example and with words, helped the Twelve exchange their previous assumptions for new understanding, and gently corrected them when they got things wrong (which unfortunately was most of the time).

Jesus' twelve disciples floundered and faltered right to the end, yet before his ascension into Heaven he trusted the building of God's kingdom on earth to these befuddled few, commanding them to follow in his footsteps and continue his work: "Go therefore and make disciples of all nations, teaching them to obey all I have commanded you. And remember, I am with you always, to the end of the age." The Apostle Paul reinforced this pattern of personal mentoring, telling the young (Jedi) Christian Timothy, "What you have heard from me entrust to faithful people who will be able to teach others as well."

The existence of a remnant of Jedi among followers of Jesus today is evidence that the early Christians were faithful to their trust; now it is our turn. If you want to become a Christian of the Jedi lineage, you will need mentors to guide you on your way. Today, a variety of organizations support you in your desire to understand faith more clearly. The pastor of a local church is responsible for providing general teaching and application from Christian scripture. Sunday School and small group Bible studies offer further instruction in the ways of the Jedi Christian. Parachurch ministries complement the church's work of equipping, as do many colleges and seminaries. They are all useful, but today we often confuse formal teaching and programmatic instruction for personal mentoring. As we have seen, the faith is taught most effectively through a relationship with an individual attentive to your development as a disciple-in-training, not through structured classroom instruction.

A mentor applies faith to your personal spiritual life as a surgeon skillfully applies scalpel to physical body. Management expert Peter Drucker tells the story of an engineering consultant called into a crisis situation to advise a local engineer on how to repair a large boiler that was about to explode. In five minutes, the consultant drew a single line on the outside of the boiler, telling the engineer his problem was located just under that line. When asked for an itemized statement for the $25,000 bill he sent, the consultant listed only two items: $1 for drawing the line, $24,999 for knowing *where* to draw the line. In the same way, a mentor applies general knowledge specifically to you, so you can develop in your practice of the faith; your mentor knows where to draw the line in your life, because your mentor knows you very well.

A Yoda who sees promise in you and is willing to invest time and attention to your development may identify you, or you may seek out a more personal and ongoing relationship for advanced study, guerilla-style, with a Yoda. What are you looking for in a mentor? You will seek a Christian whose knowledge and behavior you respect, one who will be attentive to the seriousness of your desire and dedication to seek, know, and serve the Lord of the Force.

You may worry that you will not qualify for mentoring as a Jedi in the making, that your dedication and desire may not be obvious. Obi-Wan and Yoda were both concerned when they were asked to mentor older aspiring Jedi because they were afraid they could not learn or would be too impatient to learn, as was the case with the impetuous Skywalkers, Anakin and Luke. It is encouraging to me that Jesus invited *only* those who were unacceptable to other rabbis (who probably looked at their "outward" credentials as being fishermen or tax collectors). Like Samuel, who saw the promise in David by looking on the heart and not just on outward appearance, Jesus sees your potential as an aspiring Christian just as surely as he saw the potential in a rag-tag bunch of fishermen and tax collectors. Today's worthy mentor shares this same generosity of heart and mind.

Learning to be a Jedi Christian requires more than memorizing our Holy Book and other lost sayings of our Jedi, or even finding a Yoda. Jesus' reminder that he is with us always, even to the end of the age, is a comfort, but also a call to be accountable to our Master, whose expectations have not changed and who remains ready to teach, inspire, and correct His apprentices. Aspiring Jedi, there is a lot to learn; go for it.

CHAPTER 21

Renounce the Dark Side

Never! I'll never turn to the dark side.
You've failed, Your Highness.

—LUKE, TO THE EMPEROR (*STAR WARS:*
EPISODE VI. RETURN OF THE JEDI)

Away with you, Satan! for it is written,
"Worship the Lord your God, and serve only him."

—JESUS, TO SATAN (MATTHEW 4:10)

Intoxicated with excitement after learning about the Force from Obi-Wan Kenobi, Luke Skywalker is immediately sobered by "a disturbance in the

Force" as the story he finds himself in (in the first film released, *Episode IV. A New Hope*) takes a dark turn. When he returns to his homestead, Luke discovers the smoldering remains of Uncle Owen and Aunt Beru, victims of Imperial storm troopers who carried out their murders in the service of Darth Vader, the ultimate disturber of the Force.

Immediately after Jesus' public ministry was announced, he was led into the wilderness to be tempted by the devil, and every aspiring Jedi discovers that the decision to "do, not try" will be met with the resistance of the dark side. A precondition of entering the spiritual world is renouncing the disturber of the Force (the devil, or Satan, or in Star Wars lingo Darth Vader), whether appearing overtly or subtly.

We like our villains dark and sinister in film. But "Mr. Nasty" (as my friend Nigel calls the Devil) is actually seductive, more like what the band Wilco describes in their song "Hell Is Chrome." The lead singer, Jeff Tweedy, had a long fight with drug addiction; lyrically he reveals that the devil does not appear in red but has the bright, shiny appeal of chrome. The dark side is welcoming and offers help in so many ways, beckoning us to come to a place where everything seems awesome, towering, and precise.

These lyrics reveal the lying, seductive nature of the "diabolical one," the old serpent who effectively deceives the whole world through half-truths, not through straight-out, head-on lies. As novelist Ron Hansen observes, "the devil doesn't propose temptations that are easy to resist. The devil proposes temptations that seem to be good. And you find yourself going down the wrong path for all kinds of good reasons."

This is precisely what happened with our ancestors Adam and Eve, who, though commanded not to eat fruit from the tree of good and evil, believed Satan's lie. The serpent progressively challenged Eve, first by questioning whether God had issued a command ("Did God say 'you shall not eat from any tree in the garden?'"), followed by a lie ("You will not die; for God knows that when you eat of it your eyes will be opened, and you will be like God"). The essence of all sin is the displacement of God. Eve rationalized her rebellion. "So when the woman saw that the tree was good for food, and that it was a delight to the eyes, and that the tree was to be desired to make one wise, she took of its fruit and ate." She reasoned her way into disobedience and then paid the price. Created for union with God, she was cast from the garden; created for eternal life, she—along with all humans thereafter—would die.

The dark side always aims for our destruction.
The traps are laid but concealed; Satan disguises himself as an "angel of light." One of his greatest tricks is
to make us believe in his harmless red-suited image, or
an extremely dark and obvious Hollywood one; that
way we won't see him coming.

Therefore be alert. We are at war against "principalities and powers" that seek to do us harm. Our souls
and the souls of those we love are at risk. But lest we
live in daily fear, C. S. Lewis offered a good piece of
advice: "There are two equal and opposite errors into
which our race can fall about the devils. One is to dis-
believe in their existence. The other is to believe, and
to feel an excessive and unhealthy interest in them."
We must be vigilant, but we can rest in the confidence
that our power comes from a higher source.

In whatever form the dark side appears,
the aspiring Jedi renounces the ways of
the dark side personified in the disturber
of the Force.

CHAPTER 22

Prepare for War, Live for Peace

A Jedi uses the Force for knowledge
and defense, never for attack.

—YODA, TO LUKE (*STAR WARS: EPISODE V.
THE EMPIRE STRIKES BACK*)

Peace I leave with you; my peace I give to you.
I do not give to you as the world gives.

—JOHN 14:27

The young yearn for wars while old, battle-
scarred veterans try to avoid them. When
Luke displays his eagerness to prove his skill

and become a great Jedi warrior, Yoda puts Luke's dreams of battle glory to rest, laughing and reminding him that wars do not determine a Jedi's greatness. "A Jedi uses the Force for knowledge and defense, never for attack."

So it is with Christians who strive for peace but are prepared for the inevitable spiritual war with the dark side, which seeks to destroy anyone who turns from darkness to the Lord of the Force. At Jesus' baptism the spirit descended from the sky like a dove, and a voice announced, "This is my beloved son with whom I am well pleased." But this ecstatic spiritual experience was immediately challenged by forty days in the wilderness, where Satan tempted Jesus. Nothing valuable comes without some kind of fight, and as soon as you begin the passionate pursuit of God, you enter a spiritual war.

This is a war of allegiance testing you to determine whom you really serve. This is a war of behaviors; you will find yourself doing the things you hate and not doing the things you most want to do. This is a war of attitude, with you trying to be loving, patient, and kind and instead finding your inner emotional life rife with anger, impatience, and meanness. Though your enemy is the dark side, this is a war in which you will battle the darkness within yourself and contend with it in the lives of people around you. You are in a fight to protect and purify your soul, which the dark side intends to pollute and destroy.

Aspiring Jedi, if you do not sense the power of the dark side coming against you it is likely you are not walking in the light. Until you seek, know, and use the Force, you pose no threat and the dark side will not bother with you. But I pray for courage for those of you who stand firm, resolved to live fully in the light; you will feel the full force and authority of the dark side. The philosopher William James said, "If this life be not a real fight, in which something is eternally gained for the universe by success, it is no better than a game of private theatricals from which one may withdraw at will. But it feels like a real fight."

This fight *feels* like a real fight because it *is* a real fight. At its core, life's most consequential fight is not physical, military, or political; ours is a spiritual war from which all others spring. Every war involves a contest for sovereignty, and in this war the dark side is contesting God's demand for total sovereignty. Your enemy, as the Apostle Paul reminds us, is the ultimate Vader—Satan and his forces: "For our struggle is not against enemies of blood and flesh, but against the rulers, against the authorities, against the cosmic powers of this present darkness, against the spiritual forces of evil in the heavenly places." These dark forces desire only that you violate God's first and primary commandment: to have no other gods before Him.

As Luke witnesses the massive, engulfing power of the dark side personified in Darth Vader, he wonders aloud if the dark side is more powerful. The dark side is not stronger, warns Yoda, but it is "quicker, easier, more seductive." Despite the dark side's occasional show of strength, Christians are emboldened to resist the seduction of the dark side by trusting Jesus, to whom the disciple John referred when he said, "Greater is He that is in you than He that is in the world." We know God is an active participant in this battle, as saint Thomas à Kempis reminds us. "If we would endeavor, like men of courage, to stand in the battle, surely we would feel the favorable assistance of God from Heaven. For He who giveth us occasion to fight to the end we get the victory, [and He] is ready to succor those that fight manfully, and do trust in his grace."

It is the way of the Jedi to enjoy peace though engaged in battle. In an anxious, turbulent age, God's gift of inner peace is desperately needed though rarely received. Every soul is battered and ill at ease, every spirit is restless and troubled, every human is overwhelmed with the weight of disappointments and failures; at times it seems everything in us and around us is wrong. Where can we go to find peace when our life and world are coming undone?

Jesus is peace. An angel excitedly announced Jesus' birth, saying, "I am bringing you good news of great joy for all people. . . . Glory to God in the highest heaven, and on earth *peace* among those whom he favors." Jesus calmed the turbulent sea commanding the storm, "*Peace.* Be still!" He taught his disciples to be at peace with one another, reminding them that "blessed are the *peacemakers,* for they will be called children of God." As they entered a house the disciples were instructed to first say, "*Peace* to this house." Before he ascended into heaven Jesus reassured his disciples by saying, "*Peace* I leave with you, *my peace* I give you . . . do not let your hearts be troubled, and do not let them be afraid." Though Jesus warned of wars between nations and spiritual warfare until he returns, he promised his deep, calming spiritual presence to sustain us in these times.

The philosopher Spinoza said, "Peace is not an absence of war. It is a virtue, a state of mind, a disposition for benevolence." Throughout the ages, devoted followers of Jesus have been characterized by this mysterious peace in the midst of personal or national turmoil. Among the most beautiful reflections on this deep peace is a Gaelic prayer:

Deep peace of the running wave to you.
Deep peace of the flowing air to you.
Deep peace of the quiet earth to you.
Deep peace of the shining stars to you.
Deep peace of the gentle night to you;
moon and stars pour their beaming light on you.
Deep peace of Christ, the light of the world,
to you.

When aspiring Christians read this prayer, they inevitably want to experience this kind of peace in their life. The spiritual masters teach us that this depth of peace comes through prayer and Christ's mystical presence in daily life.

One time the disciples were in a fierce storm. They panicked because they were afraid the intense winds and high waves would capsize their boat. They knew Jesus was in the boat with them, but they lost sight of the fact that Jesus, the calmer of storms, was in the boat! When they asked him for help, he gave it. In prison, Paul learned some secrets about finding Christ's peace in a bad situation. His advice seems all too simple: "Do not worry about anything, but in everything by prayer and supplication with thanksgiving let your requests be made known to God. And the peace of God, which surpasses all understanding, will guard your hearts and your minds in Christ Jesus." Sometimes we lack peace because we don't ask for it.

Through prayer you transfer your concerns to God, but Jesus also wants to transfer peace to you through his presence in your life. Earlier I referred to this presence as "mystical," because the inner presence of Christ is beyond understanding or explanation, even though Jesus' followers have clearly experienced it from the very beginning. The Apostle Paul referred to "this mystery, which is *Christ in you* the hope of glory" and said, "let the peace of Christ rule in your heart." Jesus himself said, "In me you have peace. In the world you will face persecution. But take courage, I have conquered the world!" Peace is produced by the Spirit's presence in your life; according to the Apostle Paul it is a mark of God's kingdom: "For the kingdom of God is not food and drink but righteousness and peace and joy in the Holy Spirit." Peace is a byproduct of the inner presence of Jesus, whose spirit takes residence in you.

The Jedi Christian who experiences deep peace becomes a credible peacemaker, able to approach volatile situations calmly, recognizing as Jesus did the dark side's presence and provocation in every disturbance. Such a perspective enables the aspiring Jedi to diffuse explosive circumstances by focusing on the real enemy instead of the humans caught in the grip of the dark side.

CHAPTER 23

These Weapons Are Your Life

A Jedi's saber is his most precious possession.
This weapon is your life.

—OBI-WAN, TO LUKE (*STAR WARS:*
EPISODE IV. A NEW HOPE)

Therefore take up the whole armor of God,
so that you may be able to withstand on that evil day,
and having done everything, to stand firm.

—APOSTLE PAUL (EPHESIANS 6:13)

Last year I sat in the humid jungles of Kalimantan (formerly Borneo) listening to a member
of the Dyak tribe (just forty years ago known
for its cannibalism) talk about the dramatic spiritual
growth in his village, which was a fourteen-hour hike
away. As he spoke joyfully and confidently, I couldn't
take my eyes off his sword, a work of art strapped to
his hip, yet completely functional and ready for use.

Forty years earlier, I bought a sword not unlike
his when I first visited Kalimantan as a college student.
The steel blade, forged from an old helicopter that
crashed there during World War II, was housed in a
sheath made of feathers, dyed animal hair, and intri-
cately carved bone. I loved that sword, which I brought
home and mounted carefully as a work of art in my
study, but it was stolen in a cross country move and
I hadn't seen one like it until my meeting with the
tribesman. What is obvious, of course, is that the Dyak
wore it not as an object of art but for use in everyday
life. He would hack through the dense jungle, kill and
butcher a wild boar, behead a menacing Borneo
python with this trusty weapon, and if necessary use
one like it in combat with other tribes.

As the tribesman spoke, it became obvious that he
also knew how to use the weapons of spiritual warfare.

They were not mounted in his study as a showpiece but were taken up in daily battle. He told of dramatic healings, temptations faced and conquered, doubts overcome by faith. His village's transformation from animistic cannibals to fully devoted followers of Jesus Christ did not come without a spiritual battle. The village shaman had conjured up a curse against the first Christians, begging the spirits of the dark side to attack them physically. The small group of Christians prayed and fasted, read their Bibles, and, most important, tried to show love to everyone in the village. When the shaman's own daughter became ill, the Christians prayed for her healing and anointed her with oil in the tradition outlined by James, the brother of Jesus. Her remarkable recovery was attributed to these prayers to Jesus.

As more village members came to Christ, angry tribe members began spreading lies about the Christians, accusing them of betraying the traditional spirits they had worshipped for centuries. As I listened, I felt I was watching the book of Acts unfold before my eyes; I knew these people possessed the spiritual power available to every Jedi. I was reminded that the power derives not from *knowing about* the weapons of spiritual warfare, but from actively using them in daily life.

A few days later, I was in a gift shop and saw a display with eight Dyak weapons— for the tourist, simply souvenirs to display, but for the Dyak, a means to existence. In the same way, many Christians *know about* the weapons available for spiritual battle, but the Jedi *uses* them. No longer a tourist in the spiritual world, this Christian is a combatant, using the weapons essential for life.

CHAPTER 24

Use All Your Weapons

Prepare the boarding party
and set your weapons for stun.

—DARTH VADER (*STAR WARS:
EPISODE V. THE EMPIRE STRIKES BACK*)

For the weapons of our warfare are not merely human,
but they have divine power to destroy strongholds.

—2 CORINTHIANS 10:4

A personal devil and spiritual warfare do not commend themselves in most quarters these days." So said a New Testament scholar observing the times in the late 1950s. Half a century later, after the seismic cultural shifts of the sixties, interest and belief in the demonic has never been higher. *Buffy the Vampire Slayer, X-Files, Lord of the Rings,* the *Silence of the Lambs* series, best-selling video games and songs . . . everywhere you turn in popular culture the struggle between good and evil is portrayed in classically mythic ways, with the forces of good battling various personifications of the dark side. From a young age, we identify with the ten-year-old grabbing his X-box controls, readying himself for the shooter game, and shouting, "This is not a game; this is war!"

The *Star Wars* story line takes mythic spiritual warfare very seriously and introduces a range of weapons used in such a war: the lightsaber, blaster, breath mask, and cloaking device, to name a few. Victory depends on effective use of the right weapon at the right time, and the margin for error is slim.

The Apostle Paul instructs Christians that we are also engaged in battle, against spiritual entities of the dark side. Like the Jedi knights of *Star Wars,* Paul informs us that we are equipped with our own armor and equipment for spiritual combat: "Fasten the belt of truth around your waist, and put on the breastplate of righteousness. As shoes for your feet put on whatever will make you ready to proclaim the gospel of peace.

With all of these, take the shield of faith, with which you will be able to quench all the flaming arrows of the evil one. Take the helmet of salvation, and the sword of the Spirit, which is the word of God." Paul's list was based on an even older one found in the book of Isaiah seven hundred years earlier, with God being cloaked in similar armor: "[The Lord] put on righteousness like a breastplate, and a helmet of salvation on his head; he put on garments of vengeance for clothing, and wrapped himself in fury as in a mantle."

Paul's description of the Christian's armor underscores the necessity of spiritual readiness for men and women, and though his warlike illustrations might seem macho they simply reflect his situation in life. He is writing from a Roman prison and makes allegorical use of the weapons he observes on the typical Roman foot soldier, to whose wrist he would likely have been chained when transported from one location to another:

> **The belt of truth:** Under his armor the Roman soldier wore a leather, apronlike covering to protect the abdomen and secure his tunic, freeing him from getting tangled up in his own toga. Similarly, girded with truth the Christian of the Jedi persuasion moves with confidence,

free from the entanglements of double-mindedness, able to clearly and quickly discern right from wrong and good from evil.

The breastplate of righteousness: The Jedi's upright life and unquestionable character proceed from and protect a pure heart.

Shoes to carry the gospel: In an age before Velcro, it took time to secure the jumble of straps required to fasten first-century leather sandals. The follower of Jesus is always ready to take the good news to the world because his or her feet are firmly planted in scripture.

The shield of faith: Large enough to protect the whole body, the Roman shield was constructed of leather stretched over wood and reinforced with steel on the top and bottom; when soaked in water it could absorb and snuff out flame-bearing arrows (a popular weapon in those days). So the Jedi's faith absorbs the fiery darts of temptation and protects against becoming disheartened or overwhelmed by the trials and tribulations of this life.

The helmet of salvation: Salvation means deliverance from destruction, danger, or great calamity. The Christian is *already* saved from eternal judgment, having received the gift of salvation offered by Jesus, and is *being* saved against the ongoing power of the dark side as well. Paul is saying "Get it in your head: you are saved and protected against the dark side!" New Testament scholar Markus Barth reminds us that Romans wore a ceremonial helmet when celebrating their victories over their enemies; therefore the Jedi's helmet not only functions as protection against the dark side but also symbolizes the victory that has already been won.

The sword of the Spirit: The Jedi knight's most important weapon was the elegant and powerful lightsaber, and the Christian counterpart's most potent weapon is the word of God, which functions like a sword. The writer of Hebrews said, "For the word of God is quick, and powerful, and sharper than any two-edged sword, piercing even to the dividing asunder of soul and spirit, and of the joints and marrow, and is a discerner of the thoughts and intents of the heart." Paul also reminded his young apprentice Timothy: "All scripture is inspired by God and is useful for teaching, for reproof, for correction, and for training in righteousness, so that everyone who belongs to God may be proficient, equipped for every good work."

Now picture the fully armed Jedi Christian equipped and proficient in the use of these carefully selected weapons, a battle-ready warrior. Paul completes the image with two words: *stand* and *pray.*

Like the Jedi knight, resolute Christians must take up the armor to withstand the attacks of the enemy. Jesus has already won the war; the Christian diligently wards off personal attacks in the trenches of daily battle. Our calling is to serve Jesus; we are not at war with the people of this world, but with spiritual forces that would keep us from the task of faithfully representing the loving, transforming presence of Jesus. We advance the kingdom of God while vigilantly taking our personal stand against the dark side, which attempts to keep us from faithful service to our King. We advance as servants and stand firm against our spiritual adversary.

Paul also emphasizes one final and important element in every such Christian's arsenal: prayer. "Pray in the Spirit at all times in every prayer and supplication. To that end keep alert and always persevere in supplication for all the saints." The Greek word for "all" is used

four times in these two short verses, a notable repetition
that conveys the urgency of constant communication
with the Lord of the Force. Our armor is activated
when we are actively praying. Paul wrote to the church
in Philippi, a Roman military installation, and again
placed the same emphasis on prayer, this time making it
clear that although we are suited up for battle it is God
who wins the war. "The Lord is near. Do not worry
about anything, but in everything by prayer and supplication with thanksgiving let your requests be made
known to God. And the peace of God, which surpasses
all understanding, will guard your hearts and your
minds in Christ Jesus."

Jedi Christian, you face the fiercest and
darkest of enemies, and your ally is the
most faithful, almighty God, the Lord of
the Force. Use all your weapons! Put on
all the armor—the most effective and
elegant weapons there are—and then
stand firm and pray without ceasing.

Be Strong!
The Battle
Is the Lord's!

Use the Force, Luke.

—OBI-WAN KENOBI (*STAR WARS:
EPISODE IV. A NEW HOPE*)

Be strong and courageous; do not be frightened
or dismayed, for the Lord your God
is with you wherever you go.

—MOSES, TO JOSHUA (JOSHUA 1:9)

Your training is well under way: you are involved in the uphill fight to become a Christian of the Jedi sort, and you are using the spiritual weapons in your arsenal, not just displaying them. You should never turn back from the path you are on.

By now you may be realizing that your adversary is persistent and clever; you may feel that your vulnerabilities exceed your capabilities, your enemy's experience and powers are vastly superior to yours, and if you proceed alone you will surely fail against so devious a foe. Do not be discouraged. You are serving the right and winning cause. The weapons you bear are the proper ones, and you can wield them well. The simple yet profound truth is that our efforts in service of the Lord of the Force succeed only when fronted by the Lord of the Force.

When Luke Skywalker deals the fatal blow to the Death Star, it is a one-in-a-million shot delivered by the good graces of the Force. Luke has seen a schematic of the Death Star, but he is young and his skills are not honed to the point where he can penetrate the Death Star's one vulnerability. He succeeds not because he is equal to the challenge, but because in the moment when he most needs the Force, the Force is with him.

Throughout the ages, God's people have relied on the Lord of the Force to compensate for their inadequacies and defeat their mightiest enemies. When the fearsome Pharaoh and his relentless armies pursued the outnumbered and unarmed Children of Israel across the Red Sea, Moses said, "Do not be afraid, stand firm, and see the deliverance that the Lord will accomplish for you today!" When Moses passed leadership to Joshua, the Lord spoke to Joshua and said, "Be strong and courageous; do not be frightened or dismayed, for the Lord your God is with you wherever you go." When the young shepherd boy David, armed only with five smooth stones and a sling, went up against the giant Philistine Goliath, he announced, "You come to me with sword and spear and javelin; but I come to you in the name of the Lord of hosts, the God of the armies of Israel whom you defied. . . . This very day the Lord will deliver you into my hand. I will strike you down and cut off your head, and this assembly will know that the Lord does not save by sword and spear; for the battle is the Lord's and he will give you into our hand."

We take great comfort in knowing that the Lord of the Force is on our side. But two words of caution are to be heeded. When Luke made the impossible strike in the Death Star, he knew that something beyond himself was at work; the same was true of young David when he killed Goliath. The dark side would like you to forget the source of your strength, because if you rely on yourself you will fail. Many mighty warriors have fallen over the years for just this reason.

Forgetting the real source of our victory is the first error we make in battle, but there is a second danger equal to the first. Knowing the Lord of the Force is with us, it is tempting to neglect our own disciplines and responsibilities, believing that God will bail us out of a tight spot, even if it is due to our inattentiveness to our duties as a Christian. In one of life's great paradoxes, God wants us to fully participate in this struggle, even though He does not need us to win battles against the dark side. He has designed our effort against the dark side as if we together with God form the two blades of one pair of scissors, neither operable without the other. Though we know in reality God can operate without us, we need to understand without question that we are absolutely incapable of operating without Him.

What a grand, brave heritage we Jedi Christians carry into battle, our confidence not in our weaponry, knowledge, or skills. We know we wrestle not against flesh and blood, but against powers of darkness. Our hope is in the Lord of the Force who calls us into the battle and with us will win it.

CHAPTER 26

Receive the Power

Luke, don't talk that way. You have a
power I—I don't understand and could never have.

—LEIA (*STAR WARS: EPISODE VI.*
RETURN OF THE JEDI)

But you will receive power when the
Holy Spirit has come upon you.

—JESUS, TO HIS DISCIPLES (ACTS 1:8)

W hen Darth Vader said to Obi-Wan,
"Your powers are weak, old man," he
was not only showing disrespect for
his mentor; he was undermining the Jedi's distinctive

role as a peacekeeper whose mastery of the Force enabled him to uphold just causes and fulfill his destiny. Jedi hopefuls trained for the day when a Jedi master would invite them to become an apprentice, where they would enter the trials and hone three kinds of skills: to control, to sense, and to alter.

Controlling allows a Jedi to govern his or her own inner Force. With this skill the Jedi learns to master thoughts, feelings, and actions.

Sensing helps the Jedi become aware of the Force in things beyond and outside of himself or herself, and by extension feel the bonds that connect all things.

Altering allows a Jedi to change the distribution and nature of the Force in order to create illusions, move objects, and change perceptions.

Throughout history, Jedi Christians have honed their powers of self-control, discernment, and the altering of situations and circumstances. At the outset of their journey, they receive power to become the sons and daughters of God. As Jesus prepared to return to the Father, he promised his apprehensive disciples that he would send the Holy Spirit, who would be the Christians' advocate, helping them remember the teachings of Jesus, giving them the words to say in tense situations and endowing them with unique and powerful gifts for serving the Lord of the Force.

This indwelling Holy Spirit facilitates the *inner control* often referred to as self-control. The Jedi knight is known for peace, knowledge, and serenity; the Christian is known for love, joy, peace, patience, kindness, generosity, faithfulness, gentleness, and self-control. These may seem less spectacular than the more demonstrative displays of power, but they are in fact the foundation from which all other power is distributed. St. John of the Cross recognized this spirit as the source of Christian love: "Contemplation is nothing else but a secret, peaceful and loving infusion of God, which, if admitted, will set the soul on fire with the Spirit of love." As the gardener carefully cultivates the tree over a long period of time so it will produce fruit, the Christian's daily disciplines of self-denial, meditation, and contemplation clear the way for a fuller infusion of the Holy Spirit to produce spiritual fruit in daily life. Mature Christians who master these disciplines are sometimes referred to as "full of the Holy Spirit" because their spiritual life is so obviously fertile and consistently bears fruit.

As they master the presence of the Lord of the Force in their own life, they become *discerning* about other people and events in their environment; this gives them a calm yet commanding presence. When Jesus read scripture in the synagogue, the people took notice because he spoke with authority. He anticipated the objections of the Pharisees and Sadducees, he sensed the presence of evil spirits, and he knew when to stay in or leave a village. His everyday decisions were made with a combination of calm self-assuredness and complete awareness of his surroundings. In the film *The Bourne Identity*, we learn that Jason Bourne has been trained to be aware of every detail as he enters a new situation. The Christian of Jedi aspiration possesses these same powers of observation but is also sensitized to the underlying spiritual dynamics and nuance.

Jesus told his followers to "pray without ceasing," and Brother Lawrence (1605–1691) referred to "practicing the presence of God" each moment of the day. As we cultivate God's presence, we begin to see our daily environment as He sees it. We weep in situations that move God. We become angry about the injustices that anger God. We see through the façade that people project and intuitively sense their underlying spirit. Moved by the spirit of God, we use our abilities of discernment (to see or understand; to make distinctions; to discern between good and evil and between truth and falsehood) to advance the kingdom of God toward justice and truth.

The follower of Jesus can *alter* the environment on a daily basis through a powerful spiritual presence.

When Jesus showed up, people noticed something different about him; the same is true of an empowered Christian. As we've already seen, he or she seeks a daily infusion of God's spirit, resulting in enthusiasm in everyday life. We usually associate enthusiasm with emotional exuberance, but the Greek root of the word signifies the "breathing in of God." This almost oxygenated richness inspired John Wesley to say, "Catch on fire with enthusiasm and people will come for miles to watch you burn." Enthusiasm is not the domain of a particular personality type; it is a characteristic of any person whose life channels the powerful presence of God. Reflected through a rich, unique personality, the Christian's priorities and winsome spiritual qualities alter each situation as it is encountered.

People were drawn to Jesus because of his miraculous works, but he chided them for not seeing the deeper power of God at work in less visibly spectacular but ultimately more astounding ways. For example, by forgiving the sins of a lame man prior to healing him, he put the physical miracle in perspective next to the more extraordinary and eternally significant spiritual healing. Jesus knew his very presence transformed more people than his miracles did. Likewise, Saint Francis believed the Christian's presence speaks louder than words or supernatural acts: "Preach the gospel—

and if you must, use words." Journalist H. M. Stanley's experience supported this point when, in 1871, he discovered the Scottish missionary and explorer David Livingston in Central Africa and entered the presence of a true Jedi Christian. After just a brief time with him, he said: "If I had been with him any longer I would have been compelled to be a Christian, and he never spoke to me about it at all."

Each Christian is given gifts to empower service and to alter the situation in which he or she is placed; included are gifts of serving, teaching, exhorting, giving, leading, hospitality, and administrating. Paul also mentions gifts of prophesying, healing, and speaking in tongues. A Christian might display supernatural powers in a specific situation. Samson developed superhuman strength when "the spirit moved upon him." Jesus routinely healed people, cast out demons, and on occasion walked on the water or calmed a storm. Jesus' disciples sometimes worked signs and wonders, and Peter and John called upon God to heal a lame man who then rose up and walked. These same extraordinary miracles take place today and can be used to bring outpourings of glory to God. Though dramatic, as in Jesus' day they are secondary to reflecting the presence of God in everyday life, which is a Christian's primary calling.

The Apostle Paul said, "The kingdom of God is not a matter of talk, but of power" and prayed "that you may have power with all the saints, to grasp how wide and deep is the love of Christ, and to know this love that surpasses knowledge—that you may be filled to the measure of all the fullness of God." When teaching on this passage, the "Jedi" A. W. Tozer once said, "An infinite God can give all of Himself to each of His children. He does not distribute Himself that each may have a part, but to each one He gives all of Himself as fully as if there were no others." Now, that's what I call a powerful miracle.

You've got the power; employ it for the advancement of God's kingdom.

CHAPTER 27

Power in the Blood

Make an analysis of this blood sample I'm sending you.

—QUI-GON JINN, AS HE SENDS ANAKIN'S
SWAB TO OBI-WAN (*STAR WARS: EPISODE I.
THE PHANTOM MENACE*)

But now in Christ Jesus you who once were far off
have been brought near by the blood of Christ.

—EPHESIANS 2:13

Young Anakin Skywalker's power in the force is verified when a sample of his blood confirms a higher midi-chlorian count than that of Master Yoda—a fact that stuns Obi-Wan. The Force is strong in the fledgling Jedi, with the promise of his future power conveyed through blood.

Chief among the truths my generation of Jedi Christians failed to pass on to yours is this: there is power in the blood. Turn to the ancient texts, and you will read of the spilling of Abel's blood by his brother Cain. Soon the lesson was passed from generation to generation: "Whoever sheds man's blood, by man his blood will be shed," for the "life is in the blood."

In the great Exodus of the Jews from Egypt, blood was smeared on the doorposts belonging to the Jews so God would pass over that house in fulfilling the pledge to take the life of each firstborn in Egypt. When the Jews built a Temple, the priests were given detailed instructions on how to prepare an unblemished Lamb whose blood would be shed as a sacrifice for sin. These blood sacrifices were offered in the Temple at Jerusalem until it was destroyed a few years after Jesus' bloody crucifixion.

In Christian tradition, Jesus fulfills the prophecy about a suffering messiah who would be wounded for our transgressions, and through whose stripes we would be healed. "All we like sheep have gone astray; we have turned everyone to his own way; and the Lord has laid on him the iniquity of us all." After Jesus died on the cross, the animal sacrifices were no longer necessary or sufficient, because Jesus became the sacrificial lamb. As Peter reports, "We are not redeemed with corruptible things, as silver and gold, but with the precious blood of Christ, as of a lamb without blemish and without spot." Jesus himself said, "Whoever eats my flesh and drinks my blood has eternal life." Early Christian communion celebrations even led to charges of cannibalism because they taught that the wine signified Jesus' blood and the bread his body.

All this talk of blood makes us squeamish and seems too barbaric to mention in civilized society. Surely in this enlightened age we need not fall back on primitive symbols like a bleeding lamb or a crucifix to illustrate the relationship among our stains of sinfulness, God's expectation for an unblemished sacrifice, and a pure sacrifice to stand in our stead. This is the argument of some "enlightened" moderns and postmoderns, who say that blood is now a useless and outmoded symbol: in New Testament times people could relate to blood and blood sacrifices because animal sacrifices were still being offered as part of standard religious practice, but no longer today!

Ironically, the power of blood seems more real now than ever. In a scientific age, we are more aware than previous generations were that life is in the blood, with blood tainted by diseases such as AIDS threatening life, and brutal, violent shootings bringing senseless death to a convenience store parking lot or public school.

In 2002, Clint Eastwood produced and directed a movie called *Blood Work,* the story of an FBI detective (played by Eastwood) forced into retirement for heart replacement surgery. The heart used in his transplant is from a woman victimized in an unsolved murder case, and her grieving sister convinces Eastwood to come out of retirement to identify the murderer and bring him to justice. The story weaves together a variety of potent blood images: blood work is processed at a murder scene, blood work is done to monitor the progress of a heart transplant patient, blood and organ donors make it possible for others to live, and finally a criminal sheds the blood of others. Interestingly, in the movie's opening scene, as Eastwood's character enters the bloody crime site, he is framed by the doorway while a luminescent cross shines brightly in the background. The message in this movie is clear: there is power in the blood.

In the aftermath of September 11, 2001, Bruce Springsteen linked the themes of blood and sacrifice in "Into the Fire," his moving tribute to New York City firefighters entering the World Trade Center; he vividly refers to blood-streaked skies and to the young firemen who bravely, voluntarily sacrifice their own lives.

When I first heard the Springsteen song, I was reminded of composer Gavin Bryars's haunting recording made on the streets of London. It features an old homeless man singing with sincerity: "Jesus' blood never failed me yet, never failed me yet. Jesus' blood never failed me yet. There's one thing I know, for he loves me so. . . . Jesus' blood never failed me yet." Bryars tells of leaving the tape running as he stepped out of the studio and returning to hear gentle sobbing from staff workers who overheard it.

There is something that moves us in the story of Jesus' sacrificial shedding of blood. A central theme of the Christian faith is conveyed in his moving words, "Greater love has no one than to lay down his life for a friend," and the central image of the faith is Jesus laying down his life on the cross. Again his haunting words: "No one takes my life from me; I lay it down of my own accord. I have power to lay it down, and I have power to take it up again." When Jesus laid down his life for his friends, he was including us. Even though we cannot fully comprehend it, if we trust Jesus, his blood will never fail us.

Heidi Neumark, a pastor in the Bronx, told me of visiting a "seeker-sensitive" church in a suburb where they removed the cross so as not to offend anyone. She remarked that a place like the Bronx, where blood is regularly shed, urgently needs the cross, because it serves as a reminder of the sufficiency of Jesus' blood to overcome the evil that people encounter there every day. Is not the same true everywhere on this planet? In the suburbs of the wealthy, on the dusty streets of the poor, or in war zones strewn with dead and bloodied bodies, a faith without the power of the cross is a neutered faith, one that's not worth seeking.

A cross in Eastwood's movie, a sacrifice on September 11 with blood-streaked skies, a homeless man clinging to the blood of Jesus. . . . Blood flows in life, blood is shed at death, blood is donated for those in need, and blood is one thing all humans have in common. This is a mystery handed down from one generation to the next, but aspiring Jedi of the Christian persuasion need to know: there is power in the blood of Jesus.

Christian Wisdom of the Jedi Masters

Flee the Dark Path

Now the Jedi are all but extinct.
Vader was seduced by the dark side of the Force.

—OBI-WAN, WARNING LUKE
(*STAR WARS: EPISODE IV, A NEW HOPE*)

Resist the devil and he will flee from you.

—JAMES 4:7

Yoda reduces Luke Skywalker's potential as a Jedi to one issue—his ability to resist the dark side—because once a Jedi starts down the dark path, it will forever dominate his destiny.

Today many people think there is no clear distinction between the dark and the light, seeing only shades of gray and concluding that their behavioral decisions are purely a matter of individual choice, with few consequences. Not the single-minded Christian, who understands that a path may seem right but be the way of destruction. As the Bhagavad Gita warns, "Hell has three gates: lust, anger, and greed." Similarly, Jesus' beloved disciple John describes the dark side's enticements, warning Jedi Christians, "For all that is in the world, the lust of the flesh, and the lust of the eyes, and the pride of life, is not of the Father, but is of the world."

One of the aspiring Jedi's greatest battles is within her own nature, a fight between the dark side that appeals to her fallenness and the light that can shine through her spiritual nature. The Apostle Paul describes the conflict this way:

> The works of the flesh are obvious: fornication, impurity, licentiousness, idolatry, sorcery, enmities, strife, jealousy, anger, quarrels, dissensions, factions, envy, drunkenness, carousing, and things like these. I am warning you, as I warned you before: those who do such things will not inherit the kingdom of God.

By contrast, the fruit of the Spirit is love, joy, peace, patience, kindness, generosity, faithfulness, gentleness, and self-control. There is no law against such things.

As an aspiring Jedi Christian, your spiritual nature can outwrestle the entrapments of the flesh by intentionally avoiding those behaviors from the dark side that entice you. The Apostle Paul tells his apprentice Timothy to "flee youthful lusts." This is precisely what young Joseph did when sexually tempted by the wife of his employer Potiphar; he literally ran from the room! The Apostle Paul emboldened Timothy by reminding him that the power of Jesus is greater than that of the dark side and is able to slay those temptations: "Those who belong to Christ Jesus have crucified the flesh with its passions and desires." Many aspiring Jedi have found it useful to make themselves accountable to a trustworthy friend or friends with whom they can share their temptations and failings, allowing them to pray with one another and stand together to defeat the enemy.

All of this advice is of course, easier given than followed. I may believe in God's superior power over the dark side, and I may be determined to flee temptations, but as a phrase in an old hymn laments, I am "prone to wander and leave the God I love." Fleeing is good, timeless, practical advice, but Scottish theologian Thomas Chalmers adds something to it. He advises displacing the dark side's desires with a greater devotion to God: "The only way to dispossess the heart of an old affection is by the expulsive power of a new one." Many dieters have learned that the best way to give up food that is *bad* for you is to discover food you like better that is *good* for you! As you develop an appetite for God and the good, it can displace your appetite for the dark side's offerings.

We are told that Jesus was tempted in every way we are, yet he was without sin. What did Jesus do to thwart the tempter? He recommended prayer as a preventive step, advising us to petition God to "lead us not into temptation and deliver us from evil." He also set an example by quoting scripture to the devil to overcome his temptations in the wilderness. According to Jesus, prayer and meditating on the scripture are essential elements of your spiritual diet.

A professor friend who teaches a college class on spiritual formation told me that students often complain that they aren't learning anything new about spiritual power against temptation; "We *already know* about fleeing, praying, meditating on the Bible, and trusting God's superior power," they say, "but isn't there anything else you can tell us?" Jesus warned that true Christians must be "doers of the word and not hearers only," reminding us that sometimes our solution is not new information but putting into practice what we already know. There are no shortcuts or magic bullets in our wrestling with the dark side. Our arsenal is adequate if we will use it.

The blood of the martyrs reveals the ultimate extreme to which our adversary may go to tempt us away from God and to the dark side. Even now, in Sudan, China, and elsewhere, the dark side acts through governments and militia, demanding allegiance and threatening death to those who choose God. Yet even for martyrs the severe physical consequences are offset by the spiritual rewards of obedience. Listen to the witness of Ignatius of Antioch, a direct disciple of John, who, at his execution in 107 A.D., cried out, "My desires are crucified, the warmth of my body is gone, a stream flows whispering inside me; deep within me it says, 'Come to the Father.'"

A young man recently told me his generation lacks spiritual depth because they don't face these radical, character-building, life-and-death challenges. But he is wrong. Though he likely will not face loss of physical life, he will face daily threats to his spiritual well-being. These more subtle dangers slowly erode your resolve and deaden your soul. Pornography on your computer screen, entertaining lustful feelings for a friend, letting your ambition drive you to favor workaholism over a balanced life, habitual shopping— as far as your adversary is concerned, any of these will do just fine, because once a Christian starts down the dark path the dark side will use these weaknesses to try to dominate his destiny.

Darth Vader was persistent in his pursuit of Luke Skywalker, desiring to turn him from a potentially powerful foe to a deceived ally, a relationship that parallels the dark side's hounding of the Jedi Christian. The more heroically you pursue the light and resist the darkness, the more you will be the object of assaults and temptations. There is hope. Julian of Norwich warned, "Jesus said not: thou shalt not be troubled, thou shalt not be tempted, nor thou shalt not be mistreated. But he said: thou shalt not be overcome."

Our confidence is rooted in this promise. "No temptation has overtaken you but such as is common to man; and God is faithful, who will not allow you to be tempted beyond what you are able; but with the temptation will provide the way of escape also that you may be able to endure it."

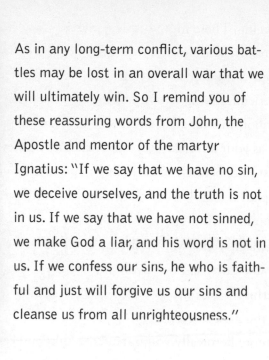

As in any long-term conflict, various battles may be lost in an overall war that we will ultimately win. So I remind you of these reassuring words from John, the Apostle and mentor of the martyr Ignatius: "If we say that we have no sin, we deceive ourselves, and the truth is not in us. If we say that we have not sinned, we make God a liar, and his word is not in us. If we confess our sins, he who is faithful and just will forgive us our sins and cleanse us from all unrighteousness."

Love Your Father

Father, please. Help me.
—LUKE, TO VADER (*STAR WARS:
EPISODE VI. RETURN OF THE JEDI*)

"Honor your father and mother"—
this is the first commandment with a promise.
—EPHESIANS 6:2

A central theme in *Star Wars* is the failed relationship between a father and his children. This is something we can all relate to, because every child suffers from imperfect parenting. With the exception of the Lord of the Force, every father fails, so as children we may refer only to an order of magnitude when bemoaning our parents' shortfalls. Fathers (and mothers) fail for the same reason children do; we are all woefully incapable of perfection.

Over the years, I've observed that our reaction to the image of God as Father is directly related to the nature of our relationship with our own parents. An increasing number of aspiring Jedi are ineffective because the fiercest enemy they face is the inner demon of a failed or disappointing parental relationship. Wounds due to some dysfunction in their family, or pain (sometimes very deep) inflicted by one or both parents weaken many aspiring Jedi. Unhealed, they can be exploited by the dark side, who will use them to produce anger or bitterness. When this happens their effectiveness in battling the dark side and serving the Lord of the Force will be diminished.

Luke Skywalker and Princess Leia's story of overcoming their lineage illustrates how any of us can prevail despite our family background, whether we suffer from mild disappointment or deep pain. In *Star Wars*, Luke and Leia bore the burden of being orphans, only to learn their situation was much worse. Not only is their father alive, he is the personification of the dark side. Ultimately Luke and Leia overcome their bitterness and forgive their father, liberating themselves from their anger, and giving their father a chance for a new start. George Lucas says that Vader was "resurrected by his children"; it is a gift only a son and daughter can give to an undeserving parent. Paradoxically, it is the one gift that will heal the son or daughter's wounds.

The *Star Wars* saga reveals a complex father-son relationship. As a young man Luke worshipped the memory of the heroic father he believed to be dead, only to hate the detestable and completely evil father he learns is alive. As an aspiring Jedi he is ruled by his passions, and when he learns the truth about his father the poisonous roots of bitterness sink deep in his spirit; his very life becomes fueled by his unmanageable anger.

Only after Luke confronts and resolves his emotions about his father can he be transformed into a Jedi. Luke takes the first step toward personal peace by accepting the truth that, through no fault of his own, he had a rotten father in Darth Vader. This requires him to let go of the idealized dream of his father as a hero. Then Luke takes another important step. He chooses to believe there is still good in his father, even asking Vader to intervene when the emperor is torturing him. His most radical step is forgiving his father, telling Yoda he cannot kill his father, and then telling his father he will not fight him. He has dissolved his hate and bitterness by releasing his inner turmoil and anger, replacing it with love and forgiveness. No longer ruled by his anger and bitter passions, he finds inner peace and qualifies for status as a Jedi.

If you have unresolved negative feelings toward a parent, this same path is available to you as an aspiring Jedi. Your healing begins when you face the truth that though every child deserves a good parent, on the scale of good to bad you got one who rates on the darker side of the scale. If this is the case, I have some encouraging news. Just as Luke and Leia transcended their parent's failures, your parents' failures do not determine your destiny, nor do they leave you without hope for a better future. If you've experienced a lack of parental love, it does not mean you are unlovable; it means your mother or father has failed, because her or his first task as a parent was to love the child. You must release yourself from any bondage imposed by your parents' failures, because their failure need not determine your destiny. Both Luke and Leia lived productive, useful lives despite their father's abandonment and betrayal; you can do the same.

Luke overcame his hatred for his father by clinging to the hope that deep down some good remained in his dad's true self; you can possess this same hope regarding your parent no matter where he or she falls on the spectrum of parental failure. For some who are deeply wounded, given the magnitude of the parent's failure, or due to lack of love, this may seem platitudinous or undoable, but it is not. Because Christians believe each human is created in God's image and has value, no one is beyond redemption—not even a despicable parent. Hoping for the best in the worst person is not easy, but it is the way of the Jedi-like Christian.

Like Luke, as a failed child you can redeem what seems like a hopeless situation by taking two more steps. You can choose to love even if you feel unloved. This kind of love is a gift God can give you; it is called *agape* love, or selfless, undeserved love. Like grace, it is unmerited and doesn't require reciprocation: "Love is patient and kind. Love is not jealous or boastful or proud or rude. Love does not demand its own way. Love is not irritable, and it keeps no record of when it has been wronged. It is never glad about injustice but rejoices whenever the truth wins out. Love never gives up, never loses faith, is always hopeful, and endures through every circumstance."

Agape love can empower you to take the second step of forgiving someone who may not want or ask for your forgiveness. This kind of love and forgiveness may never affect your enemy, or your unloving parent, but it does affect *you*. If, despite your feelings, you are able to forgive, you will be freed from the negative cancer that is eating away at you.

Fighting the inner demons born of parental failure poses the biggest challenge to many aspiring Jedi, who, like Luke Skywalker trying to levitate a craft from the swamp, may feel asked to do the impossible. Not only is it possible for you to love and forgive your parents, it is imperative for your own well-being.

In Luke's case, the story has a happy ending because Darth Vader finally realizes he loves his son and daughter more than the dark side. In his last dramatic scene in *Episode VI. Return of the Jedi,* Vader will not kill his son, nor stand by while the Emperor inflicts pain on Luke. Watching the Emperor torture his son, Vader is forced to choose between allegiance to the dark side and compassion for his son; Vader chooses his son, though it means his own death. Just before he dies, in a beautiful moment of reconciliation, Vader takes his mask off and reveals that Luke is right: there is still good in him.

Many children suffer because their parents' masks never come off to reveal their true feelings. Among the great mysteries of life is why parents who love their children are unable to express it. In Paul Simon's song "Slip Sliding Away," he tells the story of a father who longs to explain the reasons for the things he has done. The father travels a great distance and finds his son but is unable to speak. He kisses his sleeping boy and heads home again, never having talked to him. How many young men and women suffer from their parents' emotional distance? Then there is the mystery of a father who loves his child and tells her so, yet makes decisions contradicting the stated affection.

In *Episode VI. Return of the Jedi,* Darth Vader's mask comes off and he is saved by Luke's hope, love, and undeserved forgiveness; in the process Luke is also saved. I wish I could guarantee such an outcome for you with your parent if this is the struggle you face, but I cannot. I do know such an outcome is not possible if you are unwilling to believe the relationship has the potential for redemption. You cannot control your parents' attitudes and actions, but you can master your own, and in your hope, love, and forgiveness you can be healed and become a Jedi in the process.

If you've had a great relationship with your parents, be grateful. If you haven't, you must conquer your inner demons and let go of the pain. There is a final piece of good news for every one of us, even those of us who have great earthly parents. The Bible teaches that every one of us who follows Jesus has been adopted by God, who is everything an earthly parent cannot be—perfect. The adoption is a done deal; God wants such a close relationship He expects to be called *Abba*, which is Aramaic for father.

Though every earthly parent will fail, we have a Father who will never fail. Having put behind us any negative images attached to our father, we can do the right thing on earth as it is in heaven; we can love our Father.

Part 5

SERVING

CHAPTER 30

Make Your Masterpiece by Living It

I'm standing here in pieces
and you're having delusions of grandeur.

—C-3PO, TO R2-D2 (*STAR WARS:
EPISODE V. THE EMPIRE STRIKES BACK*)

For it was you who formed my inward parts;
you knit me together in my mother's womb.
I praise you, for I am fearfully and wonderfully made.

—PSALM 139:13–14

The spiritual life is about becoming more at home in your own skin," says the Quaker writer and teacher Parker Palmer. As the Jedi believed in the power of their destiny, Christians know our lives and passions are crafted by an infinitely creative Lord of the Force. By "becoming more at home in our skin" we discover our calling and make the masterpiece we are uniquely equipped to live. The Christian's call to grandeur is a duty, not a delusion.

The Talmud, the body of Jewish law, tells an illustrative story of Akiba, who on his deathbed worried aloud to his rabbi that he was a failure. His rabbi moved closer and asked why; Akiba confessed that he had not lived a life like Moses'. The poor man began to cry, admitting he feared God's judgment. At this, his rabbi leaned into his ear and whispered gently, "God will not judge Akiba for not being Moses. God will judge Akiba for not being Akiba."

Your destiny is written in your onlyness. You are the only person ever to possess your unique blend of natural skills, temperament, experiences, and spiritual sensibilities. Observe your uniqueness and understand it. Be awake and attentive to the message God is sending you through how you are "knit together," and then give it all back to the Lord of the Force. Remember the little boy who brought his loaves and fishes to Jesus, who then used them to feed the five thousand; in the same way, bring *your* loaves and fishes and offer them for their proper use, to be multiplied for the kingdom's sake.

Theologian Frederick Buechner described your calling this way: "The kind of work God usually calls you to is the kind of work that you need most to do and that the world most needs to have done. The place God calls you is the place where your deep gladness and the world's deep hunger meet." Like Eric Liddell in the film *Chariots of Fire,* who felt God's pleasure when he ran fast, your gladness originates in doing what you love to do and are gifted to do well. Celebrate your talents, and then develop and express them in your work.

Because as a Jedi you are a servant in the kingdom of God, you must go beyond simply expressing your talents; you must invest them in a mission that matters. Finding your personal mission starts by identifying the need to which you are repeatedly drawn, the societal problem you most want to see fixed, the human sorrow your gifts might help relieve. Your life's irreducible purpose is found at the intersection of your specific gifts and the needs your life's work will address.

And what of money? The Jedi Christian seeks first the kingdom of the Lord of the Force and things such as food, clothing, and shelter secondarily. The culture tells you to make career choices first and foremost on the basis of money, but there are more significant rewards at stake. We do take seriously the need to provide for our families, because as the Apostle Paul said we are "worse than unbelievers" if we fail to adequately satisfy these earthly needs, but our primary reward is the spiritual satisfaction of meaningful work that contributes to the beauty of creation and furthers the will of God. Our wealth and riches are stored in heaven, not on earth.

Jedi invest their life in work that blends expression of talents, serving a mission that matters and making adequate provision for material needs. The result is—your masterpiece, whether your work is sculpture or teaching, film or medicine, architecture or social work, rearing a family or software development. Your call to develop your gifts is where your masterpiece starts, and your ability to shape the culture around you for the glory of God is where it finds its fulfillment. In time you will also come to understand that every Jedi-like Christian has three general responsibilities in the world: to help create culture, to counter the prevailing culture, and to communicate in culture as an ambassador for Jesus.

 It is said that the world is a stage; in creating the masterpiece that is your life, the Lord of the Force is the audience who matters most.

CHAPTER 31

Loving, Transforming Presence

But this I am sure of. Do their duty, the Jedi will.

—YODA, TO MACE WINDU (*STAR WARS:
EPISODE II. ATTACK OF THE CLONES*)

And the Word became flesh and lived among us,
and we have seen his glory, the glory as of a
father's only son, full of grace and truth.

—JOHN 1:14

This morning I sat on the outside deck of a cabin in the foothills of Cle Elum, Washington, for a while not noticing four deer grazing in the tall grasses less than five feet away. Theirs was a quiet, unobtrusive presence, like that of the Jedi, who, though often silent, eventually make their presence known with words of insight or displays of power. The Christian also has a presence, the qualities of which are best understood by observing Jesus' days on planet earth.

Star Wars reveals an immense, dark, cold universe that is at times strange and foreboding, similar to the earth as seen from a distance. Only on closer inspection would an interplanetary traveler detect warmth radiating from living, breathing things. Upon Jesus' wintry arrival, the Lord of the universe found human hearts chilled by hate, loving darkness more than light, loving themselves more than others or God. God, who miraculously created the universe with a word, now willed that the word become flesh and dwell among us.

In fables the prince dresses as a commoner to discover how his people live and what they think. God was not ignorant of human ways; humans were ignorant of God's ways. So the Lord of the Force "became flesh and dwelt among us" to show us a better way, and they named him Jesus. This visitation was motivated and marked by love, for the Bible teaches that "God is love," and that he "so loved the world he gave his only Son, so that everyone who believes in him may not perish, but may have eternal life." Jesus taught humans to show mercy, kindness, and consideration for each other, giving his disciples a new commandment: that they love one another. Jesus was "moved with compassion" when he saw the human condition, observing people who were "harassed and helpless, like sheep without a shepherd." In keeping with Jesus' nature, profound yet practical love flowed from him through healing, feeding, touching, weeping, conversing, partying, eating, drinking, and teaching. Whether he ate or drank, or whatever he did, he did everything lovingly and for the glory of God.

Jesus went so far as to say that all the law and commandments could be summarized by love for God and love for neighbor, an elegant summarization based on his observation that the first half of the commandments describes ways of loving God (no other Gods, no idols, no misuse of God's name, keeping the Sabbath holy) and the second half describes ways of loving each other (honoring father and mother, no murder, adultery, stealing, lying, or coveting). Some people thought this was an oversimplification, and one group in particular, the Pharisees, were troubled because they believed God could only be pleased through perfection—specifically through strict adherence to their detailed, ever-expanding list of do's and don'ts. They felt Jesus was lowering the standards, but as anyone who tries to live lovingly will testify, by capturing the heart of God's expectations Jesus identified the highest measurement possible.

One day the Pharisees caught a woman in the act of adultery and were prepared to stone her to death, the punishment Moses allowed for violating God's law. They wanted to push Jesus' radical teachings about love to their logical conclusion, so they brought the woman to him to ask what he would do in this case. He said, "Let anyone among you who is without sin be the first to throw a stone at her." Aware of their own sin, they slipped away one by one, until only Jesus was left with the woman. The only one without sin, the only one who could rightfully cast a stone, he did not, saying instead, "Where are they? Has no one condemned you? Neither do I condemn you." Given her guilt, this act displayed God's extraordinary love and forgiveness, which is available to any human who will receive it.

There is more to the story. Jesus' presence, though loving, is also transforming and challenges us to aspire to our highest and best. Jesus turned to the woman and added these important words: "Go your way and from now on do not sin again." This story illustrates Jesus' love and compassion, but it also shows how Jesus' love is always balanced by a rigorous call to transformation.

The Apostle John said, "The word became flesh and lived among us, and we have seen his glory, the glory as of a father's only son, full of grace and truth." Jesus' love flows from his grace, and his expectation that we be transformed flows from the truth that though God loves us as we are He knows (and we know) we can be so much more. The commandments and spirit behind them reflect the truth regarding God's expectations for our better life. Each encounter with Jesus balances love and a call to be transformed to the person we should be.

Like Jesus, the Christian aspiring to Jedi ways is called to be a loving, transforming presence. The idea of a holy God actually taking on flesh and living among us seemed impossible for a religious group such as the first-century Essenes, who distanced themselves from the polluted world, moving to the caves of Qumran in an attempt to maintain their holiness and purity. Unlike the Essenes, true followers of Jesus are present in the world, as was Jesus, and unlike the judgmental, legalistic Pharisees, these Christians are a loving presence. However, a loving presence without a call to truth is unlikely to transform, and too many of us would be happy to be a loving presence without challenging people to live a higher standard and stop sinning. Such is not the practice of Jesus or the faithful Christian. Truth without grace is legalism. Grace without truth is romanticism. Truth with grace is dynamism.

Fulfilling our dynamic call to be a loving, transforming presence requires that we first allow Christ to be a profoundly loving, transforming presence *in our life*. This spirit is captured beautifully in St. Patrick's prayer for Christ's presence in our life so that we may be his presence in other lives:

> Christ be with me, Christ within me
> Christ behind me, Christ before me
> Christ beside me, Christ to lead me
> Christ to comfort and restore me
> Christ above me, Christ beneath me
> Christ in quiet, Christ in danger
> Christ in hearts of all that love me
> Christ in mouth of friend and stranger.

Aspiring Jedi Christian, may Christ dwell
intimately in you so you will be a loving,
transforming presence in the life of others
as he is in yours.

CHAPTER 32

Counter Culture Like an Alien

Someone to see ya, honey.
[lowering her voice] A Jedi, by the looks of him.

—WAITRESS DROID IN DEX'S DINER
(*STAR WARS: EPISODE II. ATTACK OF THE CLONES*)

Beloved, I urge you as aliens and exiles to abstain from
the desires of the flesh that wage war against the soul.

—1 PETER 2:11

O nce Luke signed on as a Jedi, he left his uncle and aunt's homestead in the Tatooine desert and traveled to the planet Alderaan, then to the Dagobah system where Yoda was in hiding, eventually to set up a secret base on the remote ice world of Hoth, and then beyond. Luke was getting a crash course in the Jedi lifestyle and familiarity with the phrase, "You're not from around here, are you?" The Jedi's call to the far reaches of the universe in service of the Force meant that they were well acquainted with geographic and spiritual exile. They were separated from the general population by their commitment to the Jedi Code (peace, knowledge, serenity, and service to the Force), and by their special skills and unique bond with other Jedi.

Similarly, the Christian's ancestry and calling often involve an invitation to serve God in another location and always encompass their spiritual status as aliens and exiles. Abraham, Joseph, Moses, and Daniel were all geographic and spiritual aliens. Each left home to serve God in a new land, and their lifestyle and distinct ways of living their faith separated them from the general population. Peter described Christians as strangers and pilgrims, and throughout Christian history the old traditional chorus penned by a slave in the American South has expressed both our alienation and our yearning for homecoming: "This world is not my home, I'm just a-passin' through." Jedi Christians are called to live counterculturally as members of God's kingdom and therefore as spiritual aliens, exiles, and pilgrims on this earth.

Christians in the Jedi tradition face the same choices that aliens and exiles have made throughout history as they entered a foreign culture. Recently an expert on Judaism observed that when the Jews arrived in America, they were entering for the first time a pluralistic society offering religious choice, an open society where they could ask, "What kind of Jew do I want to be?" The Hasidim, or ultraorthodox Jews, resisted assimilation and were unplugged from American society. To this day, in Hasidic communities English is a second language. Like the Amish, they wanted to be cocooned from modernity to preserve their own religious practices and ways. Other Jews moved quickly into the mainstream of American life, retaining a private identity as Jews and a public identity undifferentiated from the rest of society, accepting the idea that religion is a private matter and choosing to blend in with society.

In a classic study on the immigrant experience, *The Middle of Everywhere*, Mary Pipher reminds us, "In general, there are four reactions refugee families have to the new culture—fight it because it is threatening; avoid it because it is overwhelming; assimilate as fast as possible by making all American choices; or tolerate discomfort and confusion while slowly making intentional choices about what to accept and reject." She reports on a long-term study showing the results of newcomer adaptation. Titled *Legacies,* it concluded that the fourth option, which the researchers called "selective acculturation," was best for refugees. In selective acculturation the aliens retain their own identity while making intentional choices about what they will accept or reject in the general culture. Selective acculturation is the path of the true follower of Jesus that interests us in this discussion.

I am reminded of the artist Franco Modigliani, who as an Italian Jew in France was twice an outsider and who, after outbreaks of anti-Semitism, nevertheless persisted in introducing himself by saying, "I am Modigliani, Jew." In retaining and nurturing our distinct Christian beliefs and practices, we can find ourselves taking a stand and then feeling isolated and lonely, like the "Englishman in New York" described in Sting's song of that title. As a gay black man, the author James Baldwin found his outsider status endemic, saying sadly, "I'll tell you this, though. If you don't feel at home at home, you never really feel at home. Nowhere."

A Jedi's choices and beliefs can lead to that same dissonance and isolation from the surrounding culture, and just as ethnic immigrants seek each other out to speak the language, eat the foods, share the values of their true homeland, so Christians will be comforted and encouraged by intentional relationships with others in whom a camaraderie born of oneness in Jesus Christ can be found.

Ekklesia, the Greek word for church, literally means "called out" and refers to a gathering of Christians called out of the world and into relationship with each other. This fellowship with other spiritual aliens exiled from the broader culture is the experience of *koinonia,* a Greek word we often translate as partnership and association but that actually signifies an intimacy more closely akin to the marital relationship. We're not just talking potlucks here!

Theologian Stanley Haeurwas talks about "resident alien" Christians maintaining a sort of dual citizenship: we are residents on earth, but we are aliens here because of our overriding citizenship in the kingdom of God. We resident aliens in this sense can find *koinonia* anywhere we gather with other countercultural Christians. Ernest Hemingway said of Paris that wherever you go for the rest of your life, it stays with you. So it is with the gathering of the "called out" everywhere in the world; this is our "moveable feast." We bring the richness of our *koinonia* to all our endeavors, enhancing and transforming our daily experience and having a home wherever we find the *ekklesia.*

The church serves as Exhibit A for the values, beliefs, behaviors, and practices associated with the kingdom of God. The body of Christ exhibits Jesus' ethic in action—love, acceptance, and forgiveness—as a foretaste of the eternal kingdom of God. The *ekklesia* should represent a sharp contrast to the pagan culture around it, like light piercing darkness, or salt providing a savory accent and drawing out nuanced and complex flavors in an otherwise flat meal.

The Apostle Peter was convinced that the secular world could be wooed to the Christian's attractive and meaningful alternative lifestyle by observing the joy and peace embodied in such a gathering of pilgrims. To him the church's relevance in culture is in sharp contrast to the hollow, morally polluted, spiritually unsatisfying culture around us. Our usefulness to a fallen culture is not in adopting its language and traditions, or in becoming like it, but in faithfully representing a rich, satisfying alternative. So Peter offered three pieces of advice to the Christian among us who wants to counter culture like an alien:

1. Abstain from the immoral practices of the culture around you.
2. Conduct yourselves honorably among evildoers.

Christian Wisdom of the Jedi Masters

3. Always be ready to explain your source of hope with gentleness and respect.

The Christian seeks to fulfill what often seems a paradoxical set of relationships with culture. Though we roll up our sleeves and co-create culture like an artist, and communicate in culture like an ambassador, we also vigilantly counter culture like an alien. Peter's advice helps us sort out the ambiguities of these complex roles. As contributors to our surrounding culture, we live and work among people of all faiths, not separate from them like the Hasidim or the Amish. As ambassadors, our lives reflect the reality of a new kingdom, and we are always ready to communicate about our faith when asked. But despite our active participation in the daily activities in the culture, we abstain from those practices inconsistent with our faith, and in so doing at times we inevitably experience the isolation of the alien.

Aspiring Jedi, live as aliens and exiles, but find your life enriched by the company of friends in the "moveable feast," the *koinonia* of the *ekklesia*.

CHAPTER 33

Better World, Better Way

There is no emotion; there is peace.

There is no ignorance; there is knowledge.

There is no passion; there is serenity.

—JEDI CREED (BILL SLAVICSEK,
A GUIDE TO THE STAR WARS UNIVERSE)

So God created humankind in his image . . .
male and female He created them.

—GENESIS 1:27

Go therefore and make disciples of all nations.

—JESUS, TO HIS DISCIPLES (MATTHEW 28:19)

The Jedi were governed by a creed commissioning them to make a better world and communicate a better way of life. They envisioned a harmonious world characterized by peace, knowledge, and serenity, and even though they were often drawn into battle and known for their skills with the lightsaber, their purpose was not to wage war, but to maintain the peace and promote synchronization with the force.

Our Holy Book describes the Jedi-like Christian's two broad responsibilities on earth. First, we are to fulfill the cultural mandate articulated at creation: "So God created humankind in his image . . . male and female He created them. God blessed them, and God said to them, 'Be fruitful and multiply, and fill the earth and subdue it . . . and have dominion over every living thing that moves upon the earth.'" Second, we were given the discipleship mandate when Jesus urged his apprentices to "go therefore and make disciples of all nations, baptizing them in the name of the Father and of the Son and of the Holy Spirit, and teaching them to obey everything that I have commanded you. And remember I am with you always, to the end of the age."

The cultural mandate springs from our creative capacity, an endowment granted to us when we were created in God's image. God's activities in the first pages of Genesis are useful in understanding what we are to do on earth. There we observe God creating something out of nothing and order out of chaos ("The earth was a formless void"). We observe the quality that should characterize our work; at the end of every day God saw what He had made and "it was good." God's creative process had a relational purpose, first to communicate about Himself ("the heavens are telling the glory of God") and second to fulfill human needs ("It is not good that the man should be alone; I will make him a helper as his partner").

The banishment of Adam and Eve from the garden did not relieve them of the cultural mandate, but it did mean that though they still retained creative impulses and capacity by virtue of God's image imprinted on them their creation itself would bear the marks of the fall. So as humans began to build a culture, it was tainted by the fall. But build they did. Soon there was industry ("Zillah bore Tubal-cain, who made all kinds of bronze and iron tools") and agronomy ("Adah bore Jabal; he was the ancestor of those who live in tents and have livestock") and the arts ("Jubal was the ancestor of all those who play the lyre and pipe").

Through our work, followers of Jesus have an opportunity to bear witness to God's presence by restoring the original elements of God's creative enterprise, which means our work should be innovative, excellent, and purposeful. As writer Edith Schaeffer observes, "A Christian, above all people, should live artistically, aesthetically, and creatively. If we have been created in the image of an Artist, then we should look for expressions of artistry, and be sensitive to beauty, responsive to what has been created for our appreciation." Thus we see the younger generation of aspiring Christians intuitively grasping the significance of the creation mandate, pursing the professions, committed to character and competence, and rekindling enthusiasm for the arts. However, for this movement to succeed it needs to move beyond excelling in fallen culture, or simply imitating it, to redeeming, innovating, and remaking it. Through our work and art we participate in building a better world.

Through the discipleship mandate, Jesus followers show the world a better way of living by mentoring disciples through introducing people to Christ and his ways.

This mandate is threefold. First, we must go into all the world. Our commission is global. Recording artist Carlos Santana recently said, "I'm an earth citizen. I feel I can relate to kids in Hong Kong as well as Tijuana. Being Mexican is not all I am. I am Hebrew, I am Palestinian, I am everything. I can grasp the concept of absoluteness. I can go to Africa or Cuba or Brazil or Geneva and be part of the family, not just a tourist. I'm not one aisle in the Safeway; I'm the whole store."

Of course, you recognize that he has stolen a page from our book! Because all humans are created in God's image, we too are citizens of the earth and share a common heritage with people of every race and language; this is the basis of our cultural mandate. But Jesus also reminded us that our primary citizenship is in the kingdom of God, and this is the basis of the discipleship mandate. Two thousand years ago, "Jedi" Paul described the followers of Jesus as diverse yet unified: "As many of you as were baptized into Christ have clothed yourselves with Christ. There is no longer Jew or Greek, there is no longer slave or free, there is no longer male and female; for all of you are one in Christ Jesus."

Second, we must make disciples, through baptizing. Our task is the same as Jesus' was: to show people how to gain entrance to the kingdom of God through following the living and now-resurrected Jesus, who promises to be with us always, even to the end of the age. Theologian Karl Rahner rightly predicted that "in the days ahead you will be a mystic who has experienced God, or nothing at all." Your generation is not content to merely know *about* Jesus; you will either know him personally or you will seek spiritual satisfaction elsewhere. This dynamic relationship with the living Jesus is available, but it comes at a cost, which Jesus declared in the first century and is still the same today. Aspiring Christians receive Jesus by denying themselves, taking up their cross, and following him. Baptism symbolizes our death to self, resurrection to new life, and entrance into the family of God.

Third, we must make disciples, by teaching. The Apostle Paul describes recent converts as newborn babies; Jesus warned that they are like a freshly planted seed that must take root before growing to maturity. A disciple can be taught in a structured setting but also requires the personal teaching of a mentoring relationship. It is not enough to be intellectually informed; the maturing Christian needs to be reformed by personal application of what he has learned. As Brennan Manning's spiritual director once said to him, "Brennan, you don't need any more insights into the faith. You've got enough insights to last you three hundred years. The most urgent need in your life is to trust what you have received."

Following Jesus' example, we communicate about him and his ways in our routine conversation with our neighbors, friends, coworkers—the people we encounter in daily life. Our communication of the better way takes many forms. Just a few years ago, communicating the faith primarily involved mastering ideas and propositions and then pressing the case, as a debater or lawyer would in making an argument, or packaging and presenting it smoothly as a salesman would a product. Jesus taught in many styles, but most often he told stories. Significantly, we are again recovering the power of storytelling, communicating truth through references to our culture's shared stories—often conveyed in films, such as *Star Wars,* or through telling our own story.

Jesus knew that stories are a timeless, universally enjoyed way of telling truth while drawing people into community with each other. In an electronic age, we often get absorbed in watching highly produced stories impersonally told; but nothing can replace the power and intimacy of one person telling a story to another. I recently interviewed a man named Thomas who told me about his favorite experience as a young boy. Every evening after dinner he would gather with the rest of his family and any other stragglers who had shared the meal at a table set by his mother and presided over by his father, a masterful storyteller, who also happened to be an American literary icon. In *Down to a Soundless Sea,* his collection of short stories drawn from the memories of those evenings, Thomas observes wistfully how in the communal glow tales would be spun, skillfully, cleverly, and deftly, by his father, John Steinbeck.

We may not possess the storytelling capacity of John Steinbeck, but we each have a miraculous story to tell that also involves a father and son. It is the story of God, who loves us so much He created us in His image so we could make a better world and sent His son Jesus so we can live a better way.

CHAPTER 34

Preserve, Repair, and Make Beautiful

If there's a bright center to the universe,
you're on the planet that it's farthest from.

—LUKE, TO C-3PO (*STAR WARS:*
EPISODE IV. A NEW HOPE)

The heavens are telling the glory of God.

—PSALM 19:1

The Jedi-like Christian has a responsibility to preserve, repair, and make beautiful the environment; it is a commandment issued in the Garden of Eden and precedes the moral law we call the Ten Commandments. To preserve, repair, and maintain nature's beauty is not some fringe environmental concern. It is the will of God the creator and Lord of the Force.

I am writing from a cabin in Cle Elum again, where from a rustic oak chair at an antique dining table I have a view on three sides looking out on parched yellowish waves of wheat, then short Scotch pines, and in the distance puffs of neon white cumulus clouds spread wide and pushed high in the middle, their undersides punctured by the jagged, irregular peaks of the Stuart mountain range rising from the pine-treed foothills in the foreground. I've seen processionals of elk and coyote in the winter, but in the summer I'm more likely to see quail on the ground, red-tail hawks canvassing the open fields, and from time to time a bald eagle soaring high above, as if overseeing the proceedings below.

I find the majesty of natural beauty leads me to the Creator in a way that does not happen when I am in places crafted by humans, even places I love and enjoy like New York City or Chicago. In some places the impact of human occupation is so devastating and grotesque there is little that remains of natural grandeur. In these places, only the constellations dotting the vast unspoiled sky above remain unsullied by human tomfoolery; they tower over our polluted wasteland and point to the Great Artist, the Lord of the Force, reminding us that "the heavens are telling the glory of God."

Some Jewish traditions emphasize the preservation of God-given natural beauty as a central calling; it is clearly found in Native American theology and practice, but such a theology has nearly disappeared in Western Christianity, where progress is king and the natural order is ours to exploit and harvest without regard for the future. The Edenic mandate to lovingly care for and "steward" the earth and its vast resources has been distorted in our fallenness, used to justify exploiting and wasting irreplaceable natural treasures and life-sustaining ecosystems.

The follower of Jesus recognizes this is our Father's world and advocates and practices its proper stewardship. As Jesuit priest Teilhard de Chardin said, "The world is filled, and filled with the Absolute. To see this is to be made free." Likewise, St. Bonaventure

Christian Wisdom of the Jedi Masters

reports that St. Francis, the devout lover of God's natural creation, "sought occasion to love God in everything. In everything beautiful, he saw him who is beauty itself." When we see the natural world as the embodiment of God's glory, we are emboldened to care for our earthly trust.

Devout Christians work to preserve and create beautiful spaces of all kinds and in every place. I once remarked to writer and naturalist Barry Lopez, author of *Arctic Dreams,* how much easier it is to find natural beauty in the wild than in the city, or in our setting in Seattle, rimmed as it is with stunning mountain peaks, than in some less dramatic geographies of the United States. He disagreed, reminding me that anywhere life is found there is a native and residual splendor, if only we look for it. As if to prove Barry's point, William Least Heat-Moon wrote *PrairyErth,* a book exploring the history and wonder of a 774 square-mile tract of land in the barren, unremarkable Flint Hills of central Kansas. Heat-Moon discovered a stunning vitality and bountiful history in the area; his infectious enthusiasm for the ingenious nesting habits of pack rats, excerpts from pioneer diaries, and rich description of tall green prairie grasses in this remote landscape helped me understand the last lines of the book: "How do you know when the Prairy is in you?" "When you see a tree as an eyesore."

I interviewed him about *PrairyErth* the first
month our family moved to the flat terrain of the Mid-
west. He helped me understand locals who sincerely
believed mountains or towering trees would be an irri-
tant, blocking, as they would, their unobstructed view
of miles of prairie grasses and cornfields glowing purple
in the sunset.

I want to lovingly make a special appeal to conser-
vative Christians and the aspiring Jedi among them.
Such followers of Jesus often claim the high ground on
moral issues and their evangelistic zeal or doctrinal cor-
rectness, but they are often unconcerned about the
actual ground they stand on when it comes to the natural environment or the aesthetics of the spaces they create. One spring I participated in a conference at the
University of San Diego, a school that reflects the Jesuit
commitment to beauty. There on the hillside were wide
boulevards, fountains, indigenous trees, well-manicured
lawns, and magnificent buildings preserving a Spanish
architecture enclosing breathtakingly aesthetic interiors.
The campus was alive with the glory of God. Two days
later, I visited an evangelical campus (which shall
remain unnamed) to visit a professor friend. Stubby,
unattractive, boxlike structures appeared to have been
strewn randomly with no concern for the visual appeal
of the architecture or landscaping. One entrance to the

campus actually snaked through long stretches of barren asphalt parking lots. Perhaps their strong end-times eschatology, teaching as they do that Jesus will return very soon, explains their inattentiveness to their space now, but my physical surroundings sickened me. How can you teach the value of beauty or call students to steward the earth in such a place? You can't, and so they don't. Ideas have consequences. The Jesuits retain a theology of beauty, and their campus reflects their faithfulness to that trust; the evangelical Protestant school minimizes an obligation to preserve natural beauty, and this is reflected in the eyesore they call a campus.

Sometimes, when I think of the importance of natural beauty and human responsibility to preserve it, I think of young Anne Frank, who while hiding from the Nazis wrote these words in her journal: "I do not think of all the misery, but of the glory that remains. Go outside into the fields, nature and the sun, go out and seek happiness in yourself and in God. Think of the beauty that again and again discharges itself within and without you and be happy." I fear the day will come (and for some it has already arrived) when we step outside our door in search of beauty and will not find it, because none of the glory remains.

We have a choice. We can work to maintain natural beauty, or we can stand by and allow it to be destroyed; we can strive for aesthetic glories in spaces we create, or we can be concerned only with cost and utility. Why would we choose ugly when we could create and preserve beauty? It may seem as though I'm the proverbial John Lennon dreamer, living in a world I can only imagine, but somehow I think I'm not the only one who yearns for beauty in our places. When I think of all the spaces we have already destroyed, the ugly gashes we've cut for highways, the unimaginative utilitarian architecture dominating the American landscape, I stick by my call for a return to beauty and preservation.

Aspiring Jedi Christian, this lost saying has consequences for our enjoyment of the world and for our witness to those around us: preserve, repair, and make beautiful your environment.

Christian Wisdom of the Jedi Masters

CHAPTER 35

Live Simply, Pack Light, Hold Loose

Attachment is forbidden. Possession is forbidden.

—ANAKIN SKYWALKER
(*STAR WARS: EPISODE II.
ATTACK OF THE CLONES*)

None of you can become my disciple
if you do not give up your possessions.

—JESUS (LUKE 14:33)

If I knew you suffered from a fatal disease and did not tell you, you would think it inexcusable. Yet what if this is a disease people embrace, culture promotes, and is dear to the people who suffer from it?

I am sorry to say there is such a disease, many of us already suffer from it, and it does pose a great threat to our spiritual well-being. It distracts us from what matters, bloats us, fills us with angst, and in more severe forms is fatal. Unlike heart disease, it is not invisible; its symptoms tend to be obvious and are easily observable by friends and sometimes even casual acquaintances. Oddly enough, although there is a prescription that is 100 percent effective in treating this disease, most people seem uninterested in treating it.

The disease is called "affluenza," and it is described as "a painful, contagious, socially transmitted condition of overload, debt, anxiety, and waste resulting from the dogged pursuit of more." John De Graaf, the producer of a PBS series called "Affluenza," lists some of the symptoms: shopping fever (mall mania), credit card debt, bankruptcies, greed and envy, homes congested with stuff, a shortage of time, declining savings, an overload of possessions, consumeritis among kids (especially teens), an ache for meaning, families where money is used to express love, marriages where arguments focus on money, the feeling there is never enough. People who suffer from this disease end up working to make a dying, not a living, because no matter how much they work and earn they are never satisfied and always need more; their spirit dies a slow painful death.

Affluenza has been around for centuries. Epidemiologists searching for the first known case and cause of this disease might turn to the first-century Christian Timothy, who would direct them to the wily devil himself, saying, "Empty-handed we came into the world, and empty-handed, beyond question, we must leave it; if we have food and clothing to last us out, let us be content with that. Those who would be rich fall into temptation, the devil's trap for them; all those useless and dangerous appetites which sink men into ruin here and perdition hereafter. The love of money is a root from which every kind of evil spring."

Affluenza is an attempt to fill a spiritual vacuum through material means, so it is particularly disturbing that Christians are contracting the disease in large numbers, since affluenza is a danger to the broad culture but poses a particularly insidious threat to the followers of Jesus. A sixteenth-century Puritan, Richard Mather, warned, "Experience shows that it is an easy thing in the midst of worldly business to lose the life and power of religion, that nothing thereof should be left but only the external form, as it were the carcass or shell, worldliness having eaten out the kernel, and having consumed the very soul of life and godliness." Today's spiritual anemia is symptomatic of a bad case of affluenza.

The follower of Jesus desires only to please the Lord of the Force and is therefore eager to learn from the teaching and example of Jesus, whose teachings about material things can be clustered around three themes:

1. *Serve God, not money.* Jesus taught that we cannot serve God and money. He warned that money wants to be a master and we can serve only one master, hating the one and loving the other. Therefore he advised, "Seek God's kingdom first." When he admonished that "where your treasure is, there will your heart be also," he was reminding us that our affections drive our priorities, and our use of money is evidence of who or what we truly love.

2. *Lay up treasures in God's kingdom, not on earth.* Jesus taught that true wealth is spiritual, not material, and he urged his followers to amass their treasures in the kingdom of heaven. As an example of this, he once told his disciples to sell their possessions and give to the poor, an

act consistent with the kingdom values he was teaching them.

3. *Recognize the special challenge for the wealthy.* Jesus taught, "It will be hard for a rich person to enter the kingdom of heaven." He said this after a rich young ruler decided to keep his wealth rather than give it away to follow Jesus. He illustrated why it is reasonable to choose following him over wealth by telling the story of a merchant who searched for fine pearls and, after finding one of great value, sold all he had and bought it. Jesus and the kingdom of God are the one investment worth liquidating everything for. Jesus practiced what he preached, apparently acquiring no wealth or possessions. He did not own a home, and though he never opposed home ownership he did warn one prospective follower, "Foxes have holes, and birds of the air have nests; but the Son of Man has nowhere to lay his head."

In light of Jesus' teaching and example, the thoughtful Christian asks, How then shall I live my life?

First, you cannot choose and fully pursue the kingdom of God and the classic trappings of the American dream at the same time. Jesus desires that you live a joyful life pursuing spiritual prosperity, but the American dream tells you to expect and strive for a high-paying job, a bigger home than that of your parents, a new car every few years, the latest fashions, exotic vacations, impressive home entertainment centers, and more money and "stuff" each year than the last.

Throughout history, choosing the spiritual over the material has meant living simply and holding possessions lightly. Every spiritual tradition from Jedi to Jesus agrees on one thing, which can be summarized in the words of the old Shaker hymn: "'Tis a gift to be simple, 'tis a gift to be free." Lao-Tzu said, "I have just three things to teach: simplicity, patience, compassion. These are your greatest treasures." Gandhi added, "Live simply, so others may simply live." Thomas Celano, an early follower of St. Francis, described the simplicity and vows of poverty of the Franciscan order: "Because they had nothing, they feared in no way to lose anything."

Second, invest in the values of God's kingdom. As citizens of God's kingdom, we are to invest our time and energy in the values, practices, and concerns of the heavenly kingdom. Because Jesus so clearly expressed concern for justice and compassion for the poor, his followers have often made this their concern. St. Basil said, "If everyone would take only according to his needs and would leave the surplus to the needy, no one would be rich, no one poor, and no one in misery." In a world where thirty thousand children a day die from lack of food, clean water, and immunizations, how can we invest our resources so disproportionately?

Third, if you are wealthy, be particularly vigilant in your use of resources. Are you rich? Sooner or later each of us must answer this question, and when measured against most people in the world Americans will conclude they are very rich. So we find ourselves the target of Jesus' serious warnings about the wealthy, who, though saying they wanted to be his disciples, actually loved their money and possessions more.

John Wesley feared that love of money and material things would find its way into his heart, so he made it his aim to live on less and give away more. He told everyone that if he had more than ten pounds in his possession when he died, they could call him a robber. Near the end of his life, his journal reports, "I left no money to anyone in my will, because I had none." Though we are not to love money, we are not required to live in poverty, for Paul did admonish us to provide for our needs and the needs of our household, saying, "If you do not work, you do not eat." It stands to reason that hard-working, honest people will prosper in a system giving them the opportunity; so many of us, though pursuing God first, find ourselves with more financial resources than we might have expected. It is not the wealth that is the problem; it is how we use it.

So we who are wealthy must closely examine our actions and affections, constantly asking the tough questions to assure we are organizing our life around God and His kingdom. How do I fill my need for meaning? How does my heavenly treasure compare with my earthly one? How am I using my resources to advance God's purposes on earth? What percentage of my time and income is spent on activity relevant for the kingdom of heaven? Will I flee wealth and possessions if I find I love them more than God? Judging by my use of time and money, who or what do I love?

The call of the Jedi is to live a rich spiritual life even with few possessions, or to be good stewards of material prosperity and be content and joyful regardless of our circumstances. Novelist and theologian George MacDonald put it this way: "To have what we want is riches, but to be able to do without is power."

Jedi Christians, live a powerful life, fueled by the pursuit of God—always living simply, packing light, and holding loosely to wealth and possessions.

CHAPTER 36

The Least of These

You should be proud of your son.
He gives without any thought of reward.

—QUI-GON, TO ANAKIN'S MOTHER, SHMI
(*STAR WARS. EPISODE I. THE PHANTOM MENACE*)

Truly I tell you, just as you did it to one of the least of these who are members of my family, you did it to me.

—JESUS (MATTHEW 25:40)

Serving without thought for reward is a mark of the Jedi. The Christian also serves the disen-franchised because Jesus commands us to love them and showed us the way through his example.

225

Down-and-out "losers" who went unobserved, or worse yet were ignored and avoided by religious people, took a central place in the life of Jesus: a woman caught in adultery, lepers oozing disease, unkempt shepherds, handicapped beggars on the side of the road. In my travels to many developing countries, I've seen street scenes not that different from those Jesus saw: homeless children begging, large families crowded into cardboard shanties, teenage girls pushed into prostitution so their little brothers and sisters can eat, hopelessly deformed kids abandoned and left to fend for themselves on heartless streets.

In our own country, I've visited housing projects in the inner city, witnessed filth and drug deals; drugged-up hookers trawling the street for the next trick; an innocent child lying in a pool of blood, caught in the crossfire of gang revenge. I've seen the churches flee the urban centers and move to the suburbs, and like the religious people in Jesus' day sometimes I've looked the other way. The shortest verse in the Bible, "Jesus wept," has just gotten longer: "Jesus weeps."

What do the poor, the sick, and the imprisoned have in common?

Well, *there are a lot of them.* Abraham Lincoln said, "God must love the common man because he made so many of them," and the same can be said of the poor. The statistics are staggering. According to the United Nations,

- More than 1.3 billion people are living on less than a dollar a day.
- Half the world's population lives on two dollars a day.
- Eight hundred million people are malnourished in developing countries.
- More than 1.3 billion people have no clean water.
- Two billion people have no sanitation.
- Two billion people have no electricity.

Each of these is a person created in the image of God. The spark of life kindled in the newborn child is a possibility waiting to happen, whether born into poverty or into plenty. When a true Jedi Christian, Mother Teresa, served the poor, she saw Jesus in their faces and loved them all the more.

They are powerless. They have no leverage to gain a hearing, and no material benefit to offer those who serve them. In our own country, the U.S. Department of Labor reports that in the year 2000 "31 million people, or 11.3 percent of the population, lived at or below the official poverty level." We sometimes hear about these poor, but when did you last hear *from* them—the working poor, the victims of domestic violence, the mentally ill, or bag ladies sleeping on our streets? They appear only as statistics, political pawns moved into place in an election year, used by others but seldom given a voice themselves. Worldwide, entire regions are being written off by the West as hopeless and beyond fixing, especially where the AIDS epidemic rages and where horrendous human rights violations go unchallenged because the disenfranchised don't have a voice.

Jesus loves them. Christians are pledged to follow Jesus, who singles out the poor, sick, and imprisoned for special outpourings of time and affection. Why? He loves them. Unlike the UN, governments, nongovernmental organizations, or today's churches, Jesus is not willing that any should perish. He looks at the hapless and helpless and is moved with actionable compassion. He fed, healed, and touched the untouchables and transformed one completely unraveled soul into a well man, "clothed and in his right mind." In his first public appearance in the synagogue, he announced the arrival of God's kingdom on earth: "The Spirit of the Lord is upon me, because he has anointed me to bring good news to the poor. He has sent me to proclaim release to the captives and recovery of sight to the blind, to let the oppressed go free." When John the Baptist was imprisoned and sought news about Jesus' ministry, the message came back that "the blind receive their sight, the lame walk, the lepers are cleansed, the deaf hear, the dead are raised, and the poor have good news brought to them."

Jesus' ministry focused on the least among us, and he calls us to do the same. You'll recall that Kierkegaard was disgusted with the church in his day because it was interested in power, wealth, and cultural acceptability and had softened the gospel until it was the exact opposite of what it is in the New Testament. Are we reaching that point today?

The Jedi Christian shares Jesus' passion for what he called "the least among us" and makes a priority of incorporating these concerns, investing time, money, and influence on behalf of those who need it most. Jesus made it frighteningly clear that this is the basis on which he will judge nations and individuals:

> When the Son of Man comes in his glory, and all the angels with him, then he will sit on the throne of his glory. All the nations will be gathered before him, and he will separate people one from another as a shepherd separates the sheep from the goats, and he will put the sheep at his right hand and the goats at

the left. Then the king will say to those at his right hand, "Come, you that are blessed by my Father, inherit the kingdom prepared for you from the foundation of the world; for I was hungry and you gave me food, I was thirsty and you gave me something to drink, I was a stranger and you welcomed me, I was naked and you gave me clothing, I was sick and you took care of me, I was in prison and you visited me." Then the righteous will answer him, "Lord, when was it that we saw you hungry and gave you food, or thirsty and gave you something to drink? And when was it that we saw you a stranger and welcomed you, or naked and gave you clothing? And when was it that we saw you sick or in prison and visited you?" And the king will answer them, "Truly I tell you, just as you did it to one of the least of these who are members of my family, you did it to me."

When you as an aspiring Jedi serve without any thought of reward, you show solidarity with the attitude of humility exemplified by Christ. "Let this mind be in you which was in Christ Jesus who, though he was in the form of God, did not regard equality with God as something to be exploited, but he emptied himself; taking the form of a slave, he humbled himself." Serving the downtrodden is the closest you will come to experiencing Christ's generosity toward others.

When you pay attention and provide tangible help to the world's neediest people, you distribute more justly the resources God has entrusted to us, for all that we have is from God and belongs to Him. As taught by John the Baptist, "Whoever has two coats must share with anyone who has none; and whoever has food must do likewise."

If these words sound platitudinous, it is only because we as a society have heard and ignored them far too many times; they are from the heart of God and serve as a corrective for the selfish priorities of today's society, secular and Christian alike. Jesus identifies his disciples not only by their doctrine or fulfillment of global, large-scale schemes but also by their self-sacrifice and the attention to the hungers and needs of the world, as manifest in each individual.

Aspiring Jedi Christian, attend to the least of these; relieve the poor, the naked, the sick, and the imprisoned, for in doing so we serve Christ himself.

CHAPTER 37

Pursue God in the Company of Friends

That little droid and I have been
through a lot together.

—LUKE, ABOUT R2-D2 (*STAR WARS:*
EPISODE IV. A NEW HOPE)

And let us consider how to provoke one another to
love and good deeds, not neglecting to meet together,
as is the habit of some, but encouraging one another.

—HEBREWS 10:24–25

With Luke Skywalker, Han Solo, and Princess Leia, *Star Wars* introduced some of the great friendships in film history, with none surpassing the comedic relief and emotional intensity of R2-D2 and 3-CPO. On the other hand, the cold, unloving, impersonal Empire was built by driven individualists who never understood the synergistic power generated by this band of friends, and at one point the Emperor even mocks Luke, telling him his greatest weakness is his faith in his friends.

The Jedi Christian pursues God in the company of friends because the Lord of the Force has woven this desire in us. From the beginning God saw that "it is not good for man to be alone." We worship God in three persons, Father, Son, and Holy Ghost; our hunger for community originates in the very nature of a Trinitarian God. Humans, male and female, are created for relationship with God and each other, just as there is fellowship within the Trinity.

We aspiring Jedi are strong individuals, but we will not reach our full potential as individualists. We pursue community because God *is* community and we pursue God in the company of friends who like us, are called out of the world (remember *ekklesia*) and into fellowship (*koinonia*) with each other in the kingdom of God.

We pursue and worship God in the company of friends. The spiritual writer Richard Foster reminds us that four of twelve Christian disciplines require the involvement of other believers: confession, worship, guidance, and celebration. A glimpse of the first Jerusalem church reveals their active participatory devotion to these disciplines and to the apostles' teaching, to fellowship, praying and praising God, and eating meals together. They swarmed to each other like bees to the honeycomb.

We love and encourage each other in the company of friends. Jesus branded the church with a clear and fixed identity when he commanded his followers to "love one another," emphasizing the practical responsibilities of our love for individual people: bear each other's burdens, forgive one another, be patient and kind to one another, and confess your sins to one another. It is in community that wounded and broken people can be healed, can love and be loved. The metaphysical poet John Donne said "No man is an island," but Paul Simon disagreed in his classic 1960s lament, "I Am a Rock." Lyrically, Simon reflects on the pain and disappointments of failed friendships; in a referential play on Donne's words, he declares he *is* an island, a rock that will never feel pain and an island that will never cry. In the company of friends, pained people can be heard and loved. In the words of another classic, an Eagles song, "Desperado," pained people can be challenged to let themselves be loved before it's too late.

We are equipped for service in the company of friends. In her oft-quoted prayer, St. Teresa of Avila reminds us of another purpose for the company of friends: "Christ has no body now on earth but yours, no hands but yours, no feet but yours; yours are the eyes through which Christ's compassion looks out on the world, yours are the feet with which He is to go about doing good, and yours are the hands with which He is to bless us now." The Apostle Paul taught that the complementary nature of our talents, temperaments, and gifts means we function best together, like a body where each part needs the other and no part can say to another, "I have no need of you."

Part of our equipping comes from learning to love, accept, and work side-by-side with people who are very different from us, no doubt inspiring the old adage that "to dwell above with saints we love, oh that will be glory, to dwell below with saints we know, now that's a different story." Platitudes about love were to be tested against real people pursuing God together, warts and all. By choosing disciples with different backgrounds, Jesus made sure this company of friends would not be some comfort zone of homogeneity; his was not the company of the same, but the company of the different. For the elite in the crowd, the Apostle Paul clarified, "In Christ there is no longer Jew or Greek, no longer slave or free, no longer male or female, for all of you are one in Christ." If your allegiance is to the Lord of the Force, your cultural prejudice about gender, race, or social status can be checked at the door.

We serve as a joyful company of friends. The communitarian nature of the kingdom of God will seem like an anomaly in a highly individualistic competitive age. I love the image painted by the late Fred Rogers in a story he told about Seattle's Special Olympics. Nine contestants lined up for the 100-yard dash. At the sound of the gun all of them took off. Soon one little boy tripped, fell, and hurt his knee. He began to cry. When the other eight heard him crying they slowed down and then every one of them ran back to him. A little girl with Down's syndrome bent over and kissed the boy and said, "This will make it better." The little boy smiled and stood up, and then all nine of the runners joined arms and joyfully walked to the finish line, all finishing at the same time.

Filled with emotion, the crowd in the stadium gave them a standing ovation. Many had tears in their eyes as they clapped, whistled, and cheered for the heroic little band of friends. People still talk about that very special moment because it was a warm reminder that helping others win is truly more important than winning for ourselves, even if it means slowing down and changing our course. Such is the cooperative nature and infectious spirit of the love and joy found in our company of friends.

You may read these words and ask, Where do I find such a company of friends? My simplest answer is that you must start by being the kind of person who exemplifies the worshipping, loving, serving member of the kingdom of God described in this chapter. A pastor started his ministry in what was described as a dead church and announced that on his very first Sunday there would be a funeral for the dead church, complete with an open casket. Curious, the largest crowd in years showed up, walking single-file past the open casket. In so doing they heard a sermon without a word ever being uttered, for there in the bottom of the casket the pastor had placed a mirror. As the members looked down to see the dead church, they saw themselves.

Aspiring Jedi Christian, may your community of faith come to life, and may it begin with your renewed commitment to pursue God in the company of friends.

CHAPTER 38

Forgive, Forgive, and Again Forgive

Why do I hate them? . . . I don't want
to hate them. . . . But I just can't forgive them.

—ANAKIN SKYWALKER (*STAR WARS:
EPISODE II. ATTACK OF THE CLONES*)

Father, forgive them, for they know not what they do.

—JESUS (LUKE 23:34)

When Luke Skywalker faces his father,
he is full of anger; the Emperor urges
him to use those aggressive feelings.
Yet Luke recalls Yoda's warning that anger, fear, and

aggression flow quickly and are used by the dark side to cause us to join the fight, when the Jedi is supposed to maintain the peace. During Luke's encounter with his father, it becomes obvious that he has learned to forgive him and as a result is able to control his anger and pursue peace. In a rare display of self-control, Luke restrains himself and in so doing impresses Vader, who observes that Yoda has taught him well.

In real life the deepest disturbances in the force are due to lack of forgiveness, for without forgiveness the roots of bitterness, resentment, and anger grow deeper; the fruits born of this tree are strained or broken relationships at a personal level with friends, neighbors, a spouse, family members, coworkers, and parents, and at the global level between businesses or warring regions and nations.

When Jesus taught the gathering crowds to turn the other cheek, to forgive every day those who had wronged them, to forgive as many times as seventy times seven (evoking the need for an infinite capacity to forgive), he was speaking to people embittered by Roman occupation, living in a fragmented and racially divided society, on land of contested ownership. Israel was a volatile place, a powder keg of ancestral bitterness and war. Yet Jesus would not back off his radical teaching about forgiveness, and at the end of his earthly life he practiced what he taught, praying from the cross: "Father, forgive them, for they know not what they do."

As CNN pans the camera on a Serbian woman holding the corpse of one of her sons and she says, "My husband was killed in this war and now my son. Now I will raise his son to fight and die," we sympathize with her loss but recognize that the regrettable cycle of violence will continue into another generation. Forgiveness offers a dramatic alternative: the cycle of violence stops here. No more.

Nations are divided and at war, and so are families and individuals. As you read this, it is possible there is someone you have not forgiven. You do not want to forgive them because in your mind their actions or words are unforgivable. The follower of Jesus understands that forgiveness is a conscious, intentional, painstaking, and necessary practice; we forgive even when we don't feel like it.

Anakin Skywalker lost his identity and became Darth Vader when he gave in to hate; Luke achieved Jedi status only after he let go of his hate. Aspiring Jedi, this is one of the most difficult lessons of all for you, but it is vital, for if you do not forgive, you may be consumed by your hate and might become the enemy you so despise. Forgiveness and letting go of our hate are central to the true Christian's identity. This is why Jesus taught us to pray, "Forgive us our trespasses and forgive those who trespass against us." Karl Barth once said, "Gratitude is the precise creaturely counterpart to the grace of God," and so because God forgives us we forgive others as a reciprocal act of gratitude.

There is nothing I can say to make forgiveness easier. There are no tricks, no secrets, no magic techniques, simply the hard work of choosing to forgive. Revenge seems the logical response when you are wronged, and forgiveness and turning the other cheek are counterintuitive, but this is our heritage and practice as Christians. Forgiveness is to be a way of life, a lived reality, not merely a theological nicety, or something valued but not actually put into practice.

Few events in history reveal human capacity for inhumanity more sharply than the Holocaust, where the Nazis behaved unforgivably, crowding people into prison camps and then slaughtering them in gas chambers. Yet even in that vilest of places, the teaching of Jesus sometimes took root and displaced the spirit of hatred and revenge. Most memorable perhaps is a note found in a dead child's coat at the Ravensbruck concentration camp: "O Lord, remember not only the men and women of good will, but also those of ill will.

Christian Wisdom of the Jedi Masters

But, do not remember all of the suffering they have inflicted upon us; Instead remember the fruits we have borne because of this suffering—our fellowship, our loyalty to one another, our humility, our courage, our generosity, the greatness of heart that has grown from this trouble. When our persecutors come to be judged by you, let all of these fruits that we have borne be their forgiveness."

Forgiveness does not mean indifference to gross injustices like the Holocaust. It is an act of bravery requiring a moral strength and fortitude that may be, ironically, greatest in the face of the most profound human suffering and debasement. Aspiring Jedi, let the exemplary spirit of the note that child carried take root in your life today and bear the fruit of peace and healing for generations to come.

In Age Is opportunity

He is too old. Yes, too old to begin the training.

—YODA, ABOUT LUKE SKYWALKER (*STAR WARS: EPISODE V. THE EMPIRE STRIKES BACK*)

You who are younger must accept the authority of the elders.

—APOSTLE PETER, TO YOUNGER CHRISTIANS (1 PETER 5:5)

The system of passing Jedi wisdom from one generation to the next relied on cooperative relationships between older Jedi masters and younger aspiring Jedi. Inevitably tensions arose between young and old, as in the case of Obi-Wan and Yoda questioning the readiness of Anakin and Luke Skywalker, and Anakin's rebellion against Obi-Wan's mentoring, believing his master was envious of his superior powers.

Dissonance between young and old is woven into the fabric of human existence. It inspired Shakespeare's timeless poem in which he extols the virtues of youth over old age:

> Crabbèd Age and Youth cannot live together:
> Youth is full of pleasance, Age is full of care;
> Youth like summer morn, Age like winter weather;
> Youth like summer brave, Age like winter bare.
> Youth is full of sport, Age's breath is short;
> Youth is nimble, Age is lame;
> Youth is hot and bold, Age is weak and cold;
> Youth is wild, and Age is tame.
> Age, I do abhor thee; Youth, I do adore thee.

In contrast to Shakespeare, Christian scripture confers elevated status on the elderly, teaching us that usually with gray hair and old age come seasoning and a measure of wisdom. Nevertheless, tensions between young and old gave rise to biblical admonitions regarding relationships between young and old in the family. Children are commanded to honor and obey their parents; parents are commanded not to provoke their children to wrath.

Because the kingdom of God relies on older Jedi like Paul to pass faith on to younger apprentices such as Timothy, it is imperative that young and old learn to respect each other, because one day both will be instrumental in God's kingdom. "In the last days it will be, God declares, that I will pour out my Spirit upon all flesh, and your sons and your daughters shall prophesy, and your young men shall see visions, and your old men shall dream dreams."

Paul reminded young Timothy that if he wanted respect from his elders, he could earn it through his maturity in faith. "Let no one despise your youth, but set the believers an example in speech and conduct, in love, in faith, in purity." Peter also urges younger people to respect their mentors: "In the same way, you who are younger must accept the authority of the elders. And all of you must clothe yourselves with humility in your dealings with one another, for God opposes the proud, but gives grace to the humble."

Mentors are also instructed to behave respectfully toward their young charges. As Peter reminds them, their respect does not simply come automatically with age, or by "lording it over the flock," but by "setting an example." Paul agreed, stipulating that mentors are called to a higher standard and should be "above reproach."

"Youth culture" rules the world of commerce today, and growing old, once honored, is now feared and resisted. Entire industries promote products and services offering to retard the dreaded aging process—Viagra to retain that youthful sexual vigor, plastic surgery to keep you looking younger, hair products to hide gray or grow hair where there is none. In some industries experienced leadership is shuffled aside, not due to failure to perform but simply because our culture values youth over age. Care for the elderly has been transferred from the family to institutions where one generation is isolated from the next, to the detriment of both.

Today's popular culture repeatedly finds comedic value in the disrespect each generation shows for the other. Marketers segment people into targeted age brackets for reasons of economic efficiency. In this great cultural inversion, respect, once accorded to the elderly by virtue of their experience, knowledge, and wisdom, is stripped from them and lavished on youth, not because they have earned it but because of the perceived advantages of being young. Older people likewise are often disrespectful of the younger generation, dismissing them as slackers—indulged, irresponsible, and immature.

In many regards, churches are more influenced by the culture than by our Holy Book, shamelessly favoring inexperienced leadership over more mature, older leaders. Conversely, those powerful older leaders regularly fail to pass leadership responsibilities on to the next generation even though they are ready. Ageism cuts both ways. Churches regularly separate young and old for worship and instruction, and some emerging churches pride themselves in targeting a specified age bracket to the exclusion of others—as if people of all ages don't need each other. This is not the way of the kingdom of God, and we need to see the opportunities in people of all ages; we must also counter culture with wholehearted pursuit of intergenerational relationships.

In the church's earliest days there was a familial, mutual bond of respect between younger and older Christians. Older ones were regularly admonished to set an example for the young, while younger people were called to live up to their full potential; each group was instructed to be respectful of the other as members of God's family: "I am writing to you, fathers, because you know him who is from the beginning. I am writing to you, young people, because you have conquered the evil one. I write to you, children, because you know the Father. I write to you, young people, because you are strong and the word of God abides in you, and you have overcome."

Our failure to resolve this intergenerational dissonance diminishes the quality of our collective life in the culture, and even more so in the family of God. Younger people are missing the benefit of the wisdom and experience that comes only with age, and older people are missing the hope derived from exposure to bright, energetic, enthusiastic young people eager to meet the unique challenges of today and those of the tomorrows we will never see.

As I review my own life and ask why I feel so strongly about this subject, I realize that every good thing I've experienced personally and professionally came through the generosity of mature men and women, including my parents and grandparents, who took the time to get to know me and chose to enhance and encourage my strengths despite my obvious limitations. I recall one couple counseling me through the traumas of high school; another set aside money to help me attend college. Professors in college and seminary spent countless hours over coffee, inviting me into their home, taking a personal interest in me that extends to today. I've been the beneficiary of these same thoughtful relationships invested in my professional development.

I cannot imagine my life without these and dozens of other mature Christians, who took me under their wing, encouraged, assisted, critiqued, and helped me on the way. I believe the younger generation needs that same selfless consideration from me and my peers, and I believe we need the younger generation too. I am saddened by the disconnect between our generations because I remember what it was like when each generation served and respected the other. I think we'd all be better off if we rediscovered those ways.

Aspiring Jedi Christians young and old, show fallen culture a better way. See every age as an opportunity. Respect and value one another, invest in one another, and strengthen one another to build the kingdom of God.

CHAPTER 40

Another Chance

It is too late for me, son.

—DARTH VADER, TO LUKE (*STAR WARS:
EPISODE VI. RETURN OF THE JEDI*)

If we confess our sins, he who is faithful
and just will forgive us our sins
and cleanse us from all unrighteousness.

—1 JOHN 1:9

As a young man, everything is falling into place for the aspiring Jedi Anakin Skywalker. He is so strong in the Force that his midichlorian count exceeds that of Master Yoda. The

Jedi way is literally in his blood, and he is accepted into Jedi training with the legendary Obi-Wan. Yet over time, the hopeful promise of youth deteriorates into bitter disappointment; Anakin is transformed into Darth Vader, who, when implored by his son Luke to abandon the dark side, laments, "It is too late for me, son." Oh, the sorrow when the mighty Jedi fall.

The story of the young shepherd who grew to be King David resonates with Jedi lore. The prophets came to his village seeking a young man strong in the Lord of the Force. Though his brothers were taller, stronger, and more experienced, Samuel, the man sent by God, saw beyond David's outward appearance. Where others saw an inexperienced keeper of sheep, Samuel saw passion and a heart for the Lord of the Force. As a young man armed with only a slingshot and five smooth stones, David took on the mighty Philistine warrior Goliath and killed him. He slew his tens of thousands and inspired other young warriors to follow his lead. He was called a "man after God's own heart," and his passionate worship and seasoned wisdom, when trusted to a poetic pen, resulted in some of the finest spiritual literature ever known. His leadership, courage, and integrity foreshadowed his destiny as king, and soon he ruled in pageantry and splendor, loved by God and revered by his people. Never has one man so wholly embodied spiritual vibrancy.

Oh, the sorrow when the mighty spiritual Jedi fall. It happened when David remained in his palace one springtime, the season when kings usually leave for battle. Who knows how the dark side detects vulnerability in a human heart and subtly insinuates itself into an otherwise pure soul? From the rooftop, David's glance lingered on a naked woman bathing in a nearby villa. Bathsheba was no match for his advances, delivered as they were in a time of loneliness, for her husband was away serving in David's army. Once impassioned for God, David's heart blazed with an irrational lust, and wanting to be the sole object of Bathsheba's affections David arranged for her husband to be sent to the front lines of battle, where he was killed, clearing the way for David's now all-too-public infidelities.

The first steps down the path toward the dark side are often accompanied by a sense of release from the bondage from what seem in the moment to be archaic, irrelevant moralities serving only as barriers to our pursuit of what will truly satisfy and fill the empty space in our soul. The dark side is welcoming, warmly inviting; everything once forbidden seems so right.

Then, as the man who unknowingly drinks hemlock stirred into a refreshing drink, the symptoms of a sickness unto death manifest themselves, the slightest nausea and then shortness of breath. What seemed liberation is revealed as entrapment; what seemed like new life is now clearly a poison sickening the soul. We don't know how bad we are until we try to be good, and we don't know our own immeasurable capacity for evil until we do something really bad.

Now David, who saved others, cannot save himself from the wages of his sin, for sin always exacts a price and there are no exceptions. The first child of his union with Bathsheba dies, and David's personal vulnerability results in a professional one: he is driven from his throne and takes residence in caves while on the run. Once shielded by purity of heart manifest in his unblemished character, David is double-minded, uncertain, and unstable in all his ways. He no longer commands the undying respect of his troops, for who will gladly serve a leader who beds a soldier's wife and sends her husband to certain death in the front lines? We hear "the wages of sin is death" and seldom realize the *real* death is not physical, but rather the death of a dream, the loss of reputation, the personal knowledge that the spirit, once so vibrant within, has departed, perhaps never to return. David's sin is ever before him;

he sees it in his deteriorating circumstances each day. The sin he once romanced as a hopeful pursuit is now exposed as his death sentence.

Aspiring Jedi, this story stands as a warning to keep you from the dark side, and to remind you of the vulnerability even of the greatest among us, the Darth Vaders and King Davids. It is also a story to comfort those who fall, for though there is sorrow when the mighty fall there is also forgiveness. A broken-hearted David, the man after God's own heart, receives another chance and writes about it in Psalm 51, one of the most beautiful prayers in scripture:

> Have mercy on me, O God, according to your steadfast love; according to your abundant mercy blot out my transgressions. Wash me thoroughly from my iniquity, and cleanse me from my sin. For I know my transgressions, and my sin is ever before me. Against you, you alone, have I sinned, and done what is evil in your sight, so that you are justified in your sentence and blameless when you pass judgment. Indeed, I was born guilty, a sinner when my mother conceived me. You desire truth in the inward being; therefore teach me wisdom in my secret heart. Purge me with hyssop, and I shall be clean; wash me, and I shall be whiter than snow. Let me hear joy and gladness; let the bones that you have crushed rejoice.

Hide your face from my sins, and blot out all my iniquities. Create in me a clean heart, O God, and put a new and right spirit within me. Do not cast me away from your presence, and do not take your holy spirit from me. Restore to me the joy of your salvation, and sustain in me a willing spirit. Then I will teach transgressors your ways, and sinners will return to you. Deliver me from bloodshed, O God, O God of my salvation, and my tongue will sing aloud of your deliverance. O Lord, open my lips, and my mouth will declare your praise. For you have no delight in sacrifice; if I were to give a burnt offering, you would not be pleased. The sacrifice acceptable to God is a broken spirit; a broken and contrite heart, O God, you will not despise. Do good to Zion in your good pleasure; rebuild the walls of Jerusalem, then you will delight in right sacrifices, in burnt offerings and whole burnt offerings; then bulls will be offered on your altar.

These heartfelt words reveal a man whose heart is breaking under the weight of his own sin. He recognizes how sin's power resided in him from his youth, and that he nurtured sin in his "secret heart." He knows the pain of evil and sin and understands a truthful God is justified in punishing him. Though David will never see his reputation or kingdom restored, the punishment he cannot bear is to be cast away from God's presence. So with a broken spirit and deeply sorrowful heart, David appeals to God's steadfast love and abundant mercy to wash, cleanse, and create in him a clean heart, whiter than snow, and to put a new and right spirit within him, restoring the joy of his salvation. Then what will David do? He will get back in the fight, declaring God's praise, teaching God's ways, and singing aloud God's deliverance.

Aspiring Jedi Christian, these things are written that you might not sin, but if you do sin, God is faithful and just to forgive your sin and cleanse you from all unrighteousness. Take the word of a battle-scarred and aging Christian: you will get another chance. It is never too late.

CHAPTER 41

Touch the Sky

There is no death; there is the Force. . . .
Twilight is upon me and soon night must fall.
That is the way of things . . . the way of the Force.

—JEDI CREED (BILL SLAVICSEK,
A GUIDE TO THE STAR WARS UNIVERSE); YODA
(*STAR WARS: EPISODE VI. RETURN OF THE JEDI*)

It is in dying that we are born to eternal life.

—PRAYER OF ST. FRANCIS

Is death a beginning or an end? In Jedi lore there is no death; there is only the rejoining of life forms with the energy field known as the Force. The dance is circular, as the Jedi emerges from and returns to the force in a never-ending loop, the cycle of life.

A sharp contrast is the Jedi Christian, whose destiny is a reunion with God in an eternal place Jesus has prepared for those who follow him. In this place, often called heaven, the Jedi is not a disembodied spirit, in a vague, undifferentiated union with a "spiritual force," but dwells in a new and "incorruptible" resurrected body, an individual who having pursued God in the company of friends now enjoys eternal, in-person company with the one true, living God.

Christian scripture also describes a book of life in which are entered the names of those who will enter heaven. Unlike other myths (like that of Santa, whose list divides nice from naughty and rewards each accordingly), entrance in the eternal book of life is gained by association with Jesus, who offers life without end to those who receive and follow him. Fully devoted disciples of Jesus Christ are on the list and certain of their eternal destiny, so their life on earth is not motivated by fear of eternal damnation, but by gratitude to the Lord of the Force who offers an everlasting and abundant life. To live a rich, full life for God's glory is our chief concern, and it is interesting to imagine the epigraphs you might find on these disciples' graves, and to ponder what they tell us about those who have denied self, taken up a cross, willed one thing, and followed Jesus.

• *She won the prize.* The Apostle Paul traveled among the Greeks, who were fond of athletic competition; perhaps this is why he used vivid sporting metaphors for the spiritual life, even making reference to the Olympic wreath placed on the winner's head. "Do you not know that in a race the runners all compete, but only one receives the prize? Run in such a way that you might win it. Athletes exercise self-control in all things; they do it to receive a perishable wreath, but we an imperishable one. So I do not run aimlessly, nor do I box as though beating the air; but I punish my body and enslave it, so that after proclaiming to others I myself should not be disqualified." The writer of Hebrews picks up on this same theme: "Let us lay aside every weight and the sin that clings so closely, and let us run with perseverance the race that is set before us."

• *His roots sank deep. His tree bore fruit.* As we have already seen, the Psalmist compared the spiritual life to a tree planted by streams of water, producing fruit adorned with vibrant leaves. Jesus often used gardening metaphors, most notably in this passage where he contrasts seeds that grow to full maturity with those that don't:

> Listen! A sower went out to sow. And as he sowed, some seed fell on the path, and the birds came and ate it up. Other seed fell on rocky ground, where it did not have much soil, and it sprang up quickly, since it had no depth of soil. And when the sun rose, it was scorched; and since it had no root, it withered away. Other seed fell among thorns, and the thorns grew up and choked it, and it yielded no grain. Other seed fell into good soil and brought forth grain, growing up and increasing and yielding thirty and sixty and a hundredfold. . . .

Jesus also used the metaphor of the vine and branches, describing himself as the vine, his disciples as branches that either grow or wither up, and God as the gardener who prunes off unproductive branches for the health of the tree.

• *He touched the sky.* Jedi Christians live in constant wonder, aware of the thin veil separating this life and the next, attentive to God's accessibility and to the transitory nature of our physical world when compared to a deeper, eternal spiritual existence. Spiritual writer Kathleen Norris recounts this wonderful story of poet William Blake: "Some persons of a scientific turn were once discoursing pompously, and to him, distastefully, about the incredible distance of the planets, the length of time light takes to travel to the earth, when he burst out, 'Tis False! I was walking down a lane the other day, and at the end of it, I touched the sky with my stick.'" This is not a tale of scientific illiteracy, but of a spiritual literacy inspiring poetry, music, art, and a life filled with awe at God's imminence. Even Einstein said, "There are only two ways to live your life: One as though nothing is a miracle. The other as though everything is a miracle." No matter how much we intellectually and scientifically understand our world, at its most fundamental level all of life is a miracle, a gift from God, an opportunity to see beyond the here-and-now and into eternal glory. The fully awakened Christian lives the miracle, walks with God, and reaches out to touch the sky.

• *She sang her song.* Remember Thoreau's familiar and haunting observation, that "most men lead lives of quiet desperation and go to the grave with the song still in them." This is not the case with the Jedi-like Christian, who values the gift of life and fully invests her talents, seizing every moment to live with passion and verve, living in the same way author Annie Dillard says the writer should write: "One of the few things I know about writing is this: spend it all, shoot it, play it, lose it, all, right away, every time. Do not hoard what seems good for a later place. Something more will arise for later, something better. Assume you write for an audience consisting solely of terminal patients. That is, after all, the case. What could you say to a dying person that would not enrage by its triviality?" Having gone deeper in a superficial age, our Jedi's life is the antithesis of triviality or a "song unsung."

• *Consumed by God, he fought the good fight.* Paul carried his metaphor of spiritual warfare into his mentoring relationship with Timothy, urging his young charge to "fight the good fight of faith . . . take hold of eternal life to which you are called and for which you were made." In a touching moment, the aging Paul, nearing the end of his own journey, writes, as it were, his epitaph in a letter to Timothy: "As for me . . . the time of my departure has come, I have fought the good fight, I have finished the race, I have kept the faith. From now on there is reserved for me the crown of righteousness, which the Lord, the right-eous judge, will give me on that day, and not only to me but also to all who have longed for his appearing." Serving God was Paul's daily preoccupation from the day he encountered Jesus on the Damascus road. The complete consumption by God displayed in his life is summarized well by the Gaelic prayer:

God be in my head and in my understanding
God be in mine eyes in my looking
God be in my mouth and in my speaking
God be in mine heart and in my thinking
God be at my end and in my departing.

• *She served well.* Teresa of Avila said, "Christ has
no body now on earth but yours, no hands but yours,
no feet but yours; yours are the eyes through which
Christ's compassion looks out on the world, yours are
the feet with which He is to go about doing good, and
yours are the hands with which He is to bless us now."
The story of our life is written in the lives of those we
serve, which Mother Teresa alluded to when she
described her life as a pencil in God's hands. Jesus
came to "seek and save" the lost, but he did it by serving them and taught that, paradoxically, we lead by
serving, not by leading.

• *His was a messy, but robust spirituality.* Just
before he died the exuberant Mike Yaconelli wrote
a book titled *Messy Spirituality,* telling me it was in-
tended as a meditation on spirituality for the rest of
us: "I wrote *Messy Spirituality* because I was so tired of
reading religious books and hearing religious speakers
tell me how perfect they were, and I would end up

hearing a sermon or reading a book or going to some religious meeting, and at the end of the meeting I felt worse than when I got there because they had it all together. They had it all figured out. You know what? I'm almost 60. I've had five children. And let me tell you, I don't have life figured out yet." Mike describes what every authentic Christian knows to be true and reminds us that whatever our hope of a lofty epitaph, each of us aims high and lets grace fill the gap.

From these brief samples of possible epitaphs, we see that for the follower of Jesus death is not an end but a dramatic beginning, and life is a path to this new beginning. This Jedi finds comfort in fellowship with God, whether in living or dying. This is why Dietrich Bonhoeffer could say, as he neared his execution at the hands of the Nazis, "This is the end, but for me it is the beginning of life" and St. Francis could describe the quality of this new life now and for eternity:

> Lord, make me an instrument
> Of thy peace, where there is hatred,
> Let me sow love;
> Where there is injury, pardon;
> Where there is doubt, faith;

Where there is despair, hope;
Where there is darkness, light;
And where there is sadness, joy.
O Divine Master, grant that
I may not so much seek
To be consoled as to console;
To be understood as to understand;
To be loved as to love;
For it is in giving that we receive,
It is in forgiving that we
Are forgiven, and it is in dying
That we are born to eternal life.

And so we come to the conclusion of the collection
of lost sayings, which my generation failed to pass on
to yours.

My father was the first Jedi Christian I met, and
I would like to pass on to you one of the favorite blessings he regularly bestowed on me and his other
charges: "Now the God of peace, that brought again
from the dead our Lord Jesus, that great shepherd
of the sheep, through the blood of the everlasting
covenant, Make you perfect in every good work to do
his will, working in you that which is well pleasing in
his sight, through Jesus Christ; to whom be glory for
ever and ever. Amen."

Go forth, Jedi Christian, strong in the power of the Lord of the Force. Seek the Lord of the Force, know the Lord of the Force, serve the Lord of the Force. May peace be with you until we meet again in this life or the next.

Your servant and friend in the pursuit of the Lord of the Force, Dick Staub

NoTes

The following abbreviations are used in these notes:

KJV   King James Version of the Bible
NKJV   New King James Version of the Bible
NRSV   New Revised Standard Version of the Bible

The New Revised Standard Version of the Bible is used
unless otherwise noted.

269

Introduction

In August 1854, Houghton Mifflin's predecessor, Ticknor and Fields, published the first edition of the classic *Walden*, written by a then unknown author, Henry David Thoreau. Possibly its most famous line is the opening epigraph for this Introduction.

"The Arrangement" was written by Joni Mitchell and appears on her *Ladies of the Canyon* album (Warner Brothers, 1970).

"Listen up, maggots . . .": The character Tyler Durden said these words in *Fight Club*, a 1999 film. The screenplay was written by Jim Uhls and is based on the novel by Chuck Palahniuk.

Luke Skywalker is introduced in *Star Wars: Episode IV. A New Hope*, the first released of six in the series, but chronologically fourth. We meet Luke in the desert regions of Tatooine, where the arrival of C-3PO and R2-D2 from space, and a subsequent encounter with the reclusive Jedi Obi-Wan Kenobi, changes Luke's life radically.

Seventy-seven percent of Americans still declare Christianity as their official religion, according to the 2000 U.S. Census summary.

In an interview on the *Dick Staub Show,* market researcher George Barna stated the four reasons the younger generation are leaving their Christian roots.

C. S. Lewis took an important step toward Christianity when J.R.R. Tolkien referred to Christianity as the "one true myth." Lewis clarified this in *God in the Dock* (Grand Rapids, Mich.: Eerdmans, 1970), where he wrote, "The heart of Christianity is a myth which is also a fact."

Chapter One. Lord of the Force
"Anger . . . fear . . . aggression": We meet Jedi master Obi-Wan Kenobi in *Star Wars: Episode IV. A New Hope.*

"Walking in the light": Apostle John said, in 1 John 1:7, "But if we walk in the light, as he is in the light, we have fellowship with one another, and the blood of Jesus his Son cleanses us from all sin."

"In Jesus all things hold together": The Apostle Paul teaches this—or, as the King James Version translates Colossians 1:16–17: "For by him were all things created, that are in heaven, and that are in earth, visible and invisible, whether they be thrones, or dominions, or principalities, or powers: all things were created by him, and for him: And he is before all things, and by him all things consist."

Just before *The Fellowship of the Ring* was published, J.R.R. Tolkien, in a 1953 letter to a friend, Fr. Robert Murray, said of his work, "*The Lord of the Rings* is a fundamentally religious and Catholic work. Unconsciously so at first, but consciously in the revision. It was my desire to stay theologically orthodox that led me to avoid being too specific, despite the biblical parallels in the creation story. . . . That is why I have not put in, or have cut out, practically all references to anything like 'religion,' to cults or practices, in the imaginary world. . . . For the religious element is absorbed into the story and into the symbolism."

Tolkien's reference to Sauron's desire to be a God-King is found in J.R.R. Tolkien, "Notes on W. H. Auden's review of *The Return of the King*," in *The Letters of J.R.R. Tolkien,* edited by Humphrey Carpenter (Boston: Houghton Mifflin Co., 1981), p. 243. The full quote is as follows:

"It is about God, and his sole right to divine honour. The Eldar and the Numenoreans believed in The One, the true God, and held worship of any other person an abomination. Sauron desired to be a God-King, and was held to be this by his servants."

George Lucas's comments about God are in his fascinating interview with Bill Moyers in *Time,* Apr. 26, 1999.

Chapter Two. The Lost Sayings

For more on the Makah Indian tribe, read Robert Sullivan's *A Whale Hunt: How a Native-American Village Did What No One Thought It Could* (Carmichael, Calif.: Touchstone, 2002). This subject was also covered in an interview on the *Dick Staub Show.*

Douglas Coupland, *Life After God* (New York: Washington Square Press, reprint edition, 1995).

Read the full text of the Prodigal Son in Luke, chapter 15.

On the rediscovery of the scripture and the reaction of the Children of Israel, see Ezra, chapter 10, and Nehemiah, chapters 8 and 9.

I worked with students at Park Street Church in Boston; they also operated a student house in Cambridge, Massachusetts.

Chapter Three. Believe

"That's good. You have taken . . .": From *Star Wars: Episode IV. A New Hope.*

"Just as a candle cannot burn . . .": On-line at http://www.brainyquote.com/quotes/authors/b/buddha.html.

Lao-Tzu spoke of the Tao as an ultimate principle of the universe in *Tao Te Ching* ("The Book of the Way"), where the quotation "When the highest type of men hear Tao . . ." is also found.

"Abundant" (John 10:10); "eternal life" (John 10:28); "springs of living water" (John 4:10 and John 7:38).

"The glory of God is man fully alive": Irenaeus, *Against Heresies,* written about 185 A.D. I first saw this quoted in John Eldridge's *Waking the Dead* (Nashville, Tenn.: Thomas Nelson, 2003).

"The tragedy of life . . .": Schweitzer's autobiography *My Life and Thought* (Leipzig, Germany: Felix Meiner, 1931).

Chapter Four. "Do. Or Do Not. There Is No Try."

"No! Try not . . .": From *Star Wars: Episode VI. The Return of the Jedi.*

"The Christian ideal . . .": G. K. Chesterton, *What's Wrong with the World* (Ignatius Press, 1994; originally published 1910), chapter 5.

"Wrestles with a man": From the Torah, Genesis 32:24–25.

"Deny themselves" (Matthew 16:24); "hunger and thirst" (Matthew 5:6); "doers not just hearers" (Matthew 7:26).

"Are you going to leave too?": John 6:68.

Cortés's fleet: This is reminiscent of Steven Curtis Chapman's retelling of the story in "Burn the Ships," from his 1994 Sparrow recording *Heaven in the Real World*.

"Never! I'll never turn . . .": From *Star Wars: Episode VI. Return of the Jedi*.

Chapter Five. Wake Up. Be Healed. Be Saved.
"Help me . . .": From *Star Wars: Episode IV. A New Hope*.

Transgression of the law (John 8:34); "whoever commits sin . . ." (1 John 3:4). (The book of John is the fourth gospel in the New Testament. 1 John is one of the epistles of Saint John, also in the New Testament.)

"Be not conformed . . .": Romans 12:2.

"Giving life to all life . . .": Gabriele Uhlein, *Meditations with Hildegard of Bingen* (Santa Fe, N. Mex.: Bear, 1982).

"To journey . . .": Mark Nepo, *The Book of Awakening* (York Beach, Maine: Conari Press, 2000).

Chapter Six. Seek First
"You must unlearn . . .": From *Star Wars: Episode V. The Empire Strikes Back.*

Thomas Merton tells the story of Bob Lax in *The Seven Story Mountain* (New York: New American Library, 1961; originally published 1948), pp. 237–238.

"God is of no importance . . .": Abraham Heschel, *I Asked for Wonder* (New York: Crossroad, 1983).

"I realized that though I was not God . . .": Nevada Barr, *Seeking Enlightenment Hat by Hat* (New York: Berkley Books, 2003).

The Joan Chittister quote is from an article about her life and work in *USA Today*, July 21, 2004.

Chapter Seven. Will One Thing

You'll find useful material about Kierkegaard on the Web at http://plato.stanford.edu/entries/kierkegaard/.

"In the splendid Palace Chapel . . .": A translation of Kierkegaard's *Journals* can be found in Niels Jørgen Cappelørn, Joakim Garff, and Johnny Kondrup, *Written Images: Søren Kierkegaard's Journals, Notebooks, Booklets, Sheets, Scraps, and Slips of Paper*, Bruce H. Kirmmse, trans. (Princeton, N.J.: Princeton University Press, 2003).

"The human race in the course of time . . .": Kierkegaard, from an article published in the daily newspaper *The Fatherland*, March 31, 1855; available in Kierkegaard, *Attack upon Christendom*, Walter Lowrie, trans. (Princeton, N.J.: Princeton University Press, 1944); see also his *Either/Or* (Princeton, N.J.: Princeton University Press, 1988; originally published 1843) and *Purity of the Heart Is to Will One Thing* (New York: HarperPerennial, 1956; originally published in 1938).

"Who is my mother?" (Matthew 12:48); "Here are my mother and . . ." (Mark 3:35).

Chapter Eight. The Seeker Is Sought

"God so loved the world . . ." (John 3:16). "The Word became flesh . . ." is from John 1:14, in *The Message: The Bible in Contemporary Language* (Colorado Springs, Colo.: Navpress Publishing Group, 2002).

Parables about God's search for the lost—an old woman loses a coin, a shepherd leaves the ninety-nine sheep to find the missing one, and the Father welcomes the prodigal son—are in Luke 15.

"His father . . .": Tobias Wolfe, *Old School* (New York: Knopf, 2003).

"Oh, the deep, deep love . . .": Thomas J. Williams, *Hymns of the Christian Life* (Harrisburg, Pa.: Christian Publications, 1962), p. 175.

The 1993 Clannad album titled *Banba* includes the song "I Will Find You," featured in the 1992 Morgan Creek Productions film *The Last of the Mohicans,* starring Daniel Day Lewis.

"Amiable agnostics . . .": C. S. Lewis, *Surprised by Joy* (Orlando, Fla.: Harcourt Brace, 1955).

"One finds God . . .": Catherine M. LaCugna, *God for Us: The Trinity in Daily Life* (San Francisco: HarperSanFrancisco, reprint edition, 1993).

"The question is not . . .": Henri Nouwen, *The Return of the Prodigal Son* (New York: Image, 1993).

Chapter Nine. Enter the Cloud of Unknowing
The Cloud of Unknowing (author anonymous) is available in many editions, among them HarperSanFrancisco's 2004 edition in their Spiritual Classics Series.

The Apostle Paul refers to seeing through a glass darkly (KJV) or in a mirror dimly (NRSV) in 1 Corinthians 13:12.

A. W. Tozer's list of God's attributes is in his classic *Knowledge of the Holy* (San Francisco: HarperSanFrancisco, 1961).

Chapter Ten. Don't Miss the Big Reveal
"Lost a planet . . .": From *Star Wars: Episode II. Attack of the Clones.*

"Long ago God spoke . . .": Hebrews 1:1–3.

The concept of liar, lunatic, or Lord is developed in C. S. Lewis, *Mere Christianity* (New York: Macmillan, 1952).

Chapter Eleven. Meditate
David's hours beside still waters and in green pastures, meditating on the scriptures, are described in Psalm 23.

In *True Truth* (Downer's Grove, Ill.: IVP, 2004), Art Lindsley summarizes Lewis's writings.

"Mystical union with God . . .": James Finley, *Christian Meditation* (San Francisco: HarperSanFrancisco, 2004).

"If the doors of perception . . ." is in Blake's *The Marriage of Heaven and Hell*, plate 14, "A Memorable Fancy" (1793). William Blake (1757–1827) was a British poet, painter, and engraver. *The Doors of Perception* (New York: Dover, 1994; originally published 1954) was later the title of Aldous Huxley's essay on his experience with mescaline; and the 1960s rock group The Doors also reputedly took their name from Blake's aphorism.

In Matthew 6:9, we read what is commonly referred to as "The Lord's Prayer," in which Jesus taught his disciples to pray for daily bread and for God's will to be done on earth as it is in heaven.

"The glory that you have given me . . .": John 17:22.

"The most beautiful . . .": Albert Einstein, quoted in Kathleen Norris's *Amazing Grace* (New York: Riverhead, 1998).

On Thomas Merton's discovery, see *Christian Meditation* (San Francisco: HarperSanFrancisco, 2004) by one of Merton's students, James Finley.

Chapter Thirteen. Aim High and Let Grace Fill the Gap

"Only those who try . . .": C. S. Lewis, *Mere Christianity* (New York: Macmillan, 1952).

"Grace" is on U2's album *All That You Can't Leave Behind* (Interscope Records, 2000).

Chapter Fourteen. Trust the Lord of the Force

I first became acquainted with Mihaly Csikszentmihalyi when I interviewed him in Chicago about his book *Flow: The Psychology of Optimal Experience* (New York: HarperPerennial, reprint edition, 1991).

In 1 Kings 3:7–9, Solomon could ask anything of God, and it would be granted. He prayed, "I am only a little child . . ."

In *Star Wars: Episode I. The Phantom Menace,* Qui-Gon is talking to Anakin's mother outside the slave quarters and says to her that the young man "can see things before they happen."

Chapter Fifteen. Know and Love the Word
Bible statistics can be found in many places. The ones I cite are from http://agards-bible-timeline.com/ q10_bible-facts.html.

The whole of Psalm 119 is devoted to King David's reasons for loving the scriptures.

"But as for you . . .": These words from Paul are recorded in 2 Timothy 3:16–17.

Elizabeth Barrett Browning's classic poem is from *Sonnets from the Portuguese.* I referred to my copy of the *Family Poetry Book,* compiled by Felicity Kendal (Oxford, England: Isis, 1990).

"I can do all things . . .": Philippians 4:13.

Chapter Sixteen. Obey the Word

"You don't know . . .": From *Star Wars: Episode VI. Return of the Jedi.*

"We are better paid . . .": David Myers, *The American Paradox* (New Haven, Conn.: Yale University Press, 2000).

Bob Dylan's "Gotta Serve Somebody" is from *Slow Train Coming,* a 1979 CBS Records release, written following Dylan's conversion.

I reproduce Mark Twain's quip from memory, having first heard it from Addison Leitch in a theology class at Gordon-Conwell Seminary.

The Ten Commandments are found in Exodus 20.

"You shall love the Lord your God . . .": Jesus summarized the law in Matthew 22:37–40. Jesus' "golden rule" is recorded in Matthew 7:12. "I give you a new commandment . . ." is in John 13:34–35. Jesus told his disciples, "I give you a new commandment, that you love one another. Just as I have loved you, you also should love one another. By this everyone will know that you are my disciples, if you have love for one another."

Nigel Goodwin wanted me to see a new play while I was in London on business for the C. S. Lewis Foundation, but sadly *The Goat, Or Who Is Sylvia?* had finished its run two weeks earlier. I bought the script (New York: Methuen, 2004) and was stunned by the insights of this 2002 Tony Award winner for best play.

"See, I have set before you today . . .": Moses summarizes his message regarding the decision the next generation faces in Deuteronomy 30:11–20.

"I know the power . . .": Teresa of Avila, mystic and teacher, 1582; found at www.worldofquotes.com.

"The greatest thing . . .": William Barclay, *The Mind of Jesus* (San Francisco: HarperSanFrancisco, 1976).

Chapter Seventeen. Believe to See
"Your eyes can deceive you . . .": From *Star Wars: Episode IV. A New Hope.*

"The assurance of things hoped for . . .": Hebrews 11:1.

"Conquered kingdoms, administered justice . . .": Hebrews 11:32 and following.

"Belief, doubt . . .": Kathleen Norris, *Amazing Grace* (New York: Riverhead, 1998).

"Good sermon, Reverend . . .": cartoon in the *New Yorker,* Dec. 1, 2003.

"Faith is to believe . . .": I found this quote from Augustine at http://www.quotedb.com/quotes/215).

"In faith there is enough light . . .": This quote from Blaise Pascal can be found on-line at http://www.brainyquote.com/quotes/authors/b/blaise_pascal.html.

"I believe, help my unbelief . . .": Mark 9:24.

"To one who has faith . . .": This quote from Thomas Aquinas can be found at http://en.thinkexist.com/quotes/st._thomas_aquinas/3.html.

Norman Mailer's comments are from a personal conversation after I interviewed him in Chicago about his 1998 book *Time of Our Time.*

Chapter Eighteen. The Lord of the Force You Are Not

Anakin Skywalker exposes his anger and frustration in

a conversation with Senator Padmé in *Star Wars: Episode II. Attack of the Clones.*

"A person will worship something . . ." and "We may think . . .": These Ralph Waldo Emerson quotes were found at http://www.wisdomquotes.com/001797.html.

"The universe has . . .": This Aleksandr Solzhenitsyn quote was found at http://en.thinkexist.com/quotation/ The_Universe_has_as_many_different_centers_as/ 169863.html.

On Adam and Eve's marital stress, see Genesis 3; their son's murdering his brother is in Genesis 4. On the inclination of human hearts being "only evil continually," see Genesis 6.

I've heard this Abraham Kuyper quote many times; the first time was at a 1998 talk by Peter Kuzmik at a Lausanne Committee for World Evangelization event in Singapore.

"God is made to wait . . .": A. W. Tozer, *Man: The Dwelling Place of God* (Harrisburg, Pa.: Christian Publications, 1966).

Chapter Nineteen. Changed

"I appeal to you therefore . . .": Romans 12:1–3.

"Do nothing from selfish ambition . . .": Thus Paul describes Jesus' humility in the famous "kenosis" passage in Philippians 2.

"For as in one body . . .": 1 Corinthians 12:12–30.

"Let love be genuine . . .": Romans 12:9–18.

"If anyone is in Christ . . .": 2 Corinthians 5:17.

Entertainment Weekly (Sept. 24, 2004) carried an interesting analysis of Lucas's remake of *Star Wars* in the final cut of *Episode IV. A New Hope* (the first film released), involving a question about whether Solo or Greedo shot first.

"Who will separate us . . .": Romans 8:35–39.

Chapter Twenty. "Always Two There Are, a Master and an Apprentice"

"The next day John again was standing . . .": John 1:35–42.

"Hear, O Israel . . .": Deuteronomy 6:3–9.

What is often called Jesus' "great commission" ("Go therefore . . .") is found in Matthew 28:19–20.

"What you have heard . . .": 2 Timothy 2:2.

I heard the story of the big bill for "knowing where to draw the line" from management expert Peter Drucker.

The account of Samuel seeing David's potential is in 1 Samuel 16:6–7.

Chapter Twenty-One. Renounce the Dark Side
In Matthew 4:1–11, we read about Jesus being led into the wilderness to be tempted by the devil.

"Hell Is Chrome," from Wilco's album *A Ghost Is Born* (Nonesuch, 2004).

Novelist Ron Hansen made the observations about the dark side in an interview on the *Dick Staub Show* in 2003.

"The tree was good for food . . .": Genesis 3.

"Principalities and powers . . .": Ephesians 6:12.

"There are two equal . . .": C. S. Lewis, *The Screwtape Letters* (New York: Macmillan, 1982).

Chapter Twenty-Two. Prepare for War, Live for Peace

"This is my beloved son . . .": Matthew 3:17.

"If this life be not a real fight . . .": William James, in Hibbert Lectures at Manchester College, Oxford University, 1908.

"For our struggle . . .": Ephesians 6:12–16.

"The dark side is not stronger": From *Star Wars: Episode V. The Empire Strikes Back.*

"Greater is He . . .": 1 John 4:4.

"If we would endeavor . . .": Thomas à Kempis, *Imitation of Christ* (Spiritual Classics edition; New York: Vintage, 1998).

"I am bringing you good news . . ." (Luke 2:14). Jesus calmed the sea: "*Peace.* Be still!" in Mark 4:39. "Blessed are the *peacemakers* . . ." (Matthew 5:9). "*Peace* to this house" (Luke 10:5). "*Peace* I leave with you . . ." (John 14:27).

The Dutch Jewish philosopher (1632–1677) Baruch Spinoza said, "Peace is not an absence of war. . . ." *Spinoza Reader* (Princeton, N.J.: Princeton University Press, 1994).

I am a sucker for John Rutter's music; the lyrics for the Gaelic prayer are from his 1988 *Gloria* (Collegium).

"Do not worry about anything . . .": Philippians 4:6–7.

"This mystery, which is Christ in you . . ." (Colossians 1:27). "Let the peace of Christ . . ." (Colossians 3:15). "In me you have peace . . ." (John 16:33). "For the kingdom of God . . ." (Galatians 5:22).

Chapter Twenty-Three. These Weapons Are Your Life
"Take up the whole armor of God . . .": Ephesians 6:11.

The Dyak story is a personal one. I first visited Kalimantan in 1966 when I was a student and guest of the Christian and Missionary Alliance visiting their work

in East Kalimantan. I returned to visit West Kalimantan in 2002 as a guest of the Bible League.

Chapter Twenty-Four. Use All Your Weapons
"A personal devil . . .": F. Foulkes, *Tyndale Bible Com-
mentary on Ephesians* (Grand Rapids, Mich.: Tyndale
Press, 1963).

"Fasten the belt of truth . . .": Ephesians 6:10–20.

"[The Lord] put on righteousness . . .": Isaiah 59:16–18.

The concept of the Roman ceremonial helmet is from
Markus Barth's *Anchor Bible Commentary on Ephesians*
(New York: Doubleday, 1974).

"For the word of God is quick . . ." (Hebrews 4:12,
KJV). "All scripture is inspired by God . . ." (2 Timothy 3:16).

"Pray in the Spirit . . ." (Ephesians 6:18). "The Lord is
near . . ." (Philippians 4:5-7).

**Chapter Twenty-Five. Be Strong! The Battle
Is the Lord's!**
Luke Skywalker's one-in-a-million fatal shot to the
Death Star occurs in *Star Wars: Episode IV. A New Hope.*

"Do not be afraid, stand firm . . ." (Exodus 14:14).
"Be strong and courageous . . ." (Joshua 1:5–9).

"You come to me with sword . . .": 1 Samuel
17:45–47.

Chapter Twenty-Six. Receive the Power
In *Star Wars: Episode IV. A New Hope,* Darth Vader said
to Obi-Wan, "your powers are weak, old man." For a
complete description of Jedi use of the Force, see *A
Guide to the Star Wars Universe* by Bill Slavicsek (New
York: Ballantine, 3rd edition, 2000). You'll find
descriptions of the *controlling, sensing,* and *altering*
skills discussed in the chapter.

The Jedi knight's peace, knowledge, and serenity: see
the Jedi Creed in *A Guide to the Star Wars Universe.*
The Christian's virtues are from Galatians 5:22–23.

St. John of the Cross (1542–1591) wrote three books
focused on contemplation: *Ascent of Mount Carmel,* its
companion piece *Dark Night of the Soul,* and *Living
Flame of Love.* The last one is the source of the quote
on contemplation in the chapter.

In Mark 1:27 we observe that when Jesus read scripture in the synagogue, people took notice because of his authority.

The Bourne Identity is a Universal Pictures adaptation of Robert Ludlum's best-selling novel of the same title.

In *The Practice of the Presence of God* (New Kensington, Pa.: Whitaker House, 1982), Brother Lawrence referred to "practicing the presence of God" each moment of the day.

"Catch on fire . . .": Fire was an important theme for the prolific John Wesley (1703–1791). This quote is at http://www.brainyquote.com/quotes/quotes/j/johnwesley134868.html.

"If I had been with him any longer . . .": This story of Stanley and Livingstone is from a William Barclay commentary.

"The kingdom of God . . ." (1 Corinthians 4:20). "That you may have power . . ." (Ephesians 3:19–20).

"An infinite God can give . . .": A. W. Tozer quote from www.brainyquote.com/quotes/authors/a/a_w_tozer.html.

Chapter Twenty-Seven. Power in the Blood

"Whoever sheds man's blood . . .": Genesis 9:3–6.

On the Hebrews' homes being spared, see Exodus 12. On preparing an unblemished lamb, see Exodus 23–30.

"All we like sheep . . ." (Isaiah 53:4-7). "We are not redeemed . . ." (1 Peter 1:18–21). In John 6:51, Jesus said, "I am the living bread . . ."

Early Christian communion celebrations even led to charges of cannibalism because of Jesus' comments about his body and blood represented in the meal. In *A New Eusebius* (edited by J. Stevenson; London: SPCK, 1957), a collection of excerpted documents about church history dating from 337 A.D. and earlier, we read that Caecilius described the early Christians as a "rabble if impious conspirators; at their nocturnal gatherings, solemn fasts, and barbarous meals the bond of union is not any sacred rite but a crime. They are a secret tribe that lurks in darkness and shuns the light, silent in public, chattering in corners."

Blood Work was released by Warner Brothers in 2002.

The Rising, a 2002 Sony release, included the song "Into the Fire."

Gavin Bryar's haunting recording is a Philips release from 1993 titled *Jesus' Blood Never Failed Me Yet.*

"No one takes my life from me . . .": John 10:17–18

Heidi Neumark, *Breathing Space: A Spiritual Journey in the South Bronx* (Boston: Beacon Press, 2003).

Chapter Twenty-Eight. Flee the Dark Path
"For all that is in the world . . .": 1 John 2:16, KJV.

"The works of the flesh are obvious . . .": Galatians 5:19–26.

"Flee youthful lusts": 2 Timothy 2:22.

"Those who belong to Christ Jesus . . .": Galatians 5:22.

"Prone to wander . . .": Robert Robinson, "Come Thou Fount" (1758; *Hymns of the Christian Life.* Harrisburg, Pa.: Christian Publications, 1962).

"The only way to dispossess . . .": Scottish theologian Thomas Chalmers (1780–1847) delivered these words in a famous sermon titled *The Expulsive Power of a New Affection.*

"My desires are crucified . . .": In *Prayers of the Martyrs* (Grand Rapids, Mich.: Zondervan, 1991).

"Jesus said not . . .": Julian of Norwich, *Revelations of Divine Love* (New York: Penguin, 1999), chapter 68.

"If we say that we have no sin": 1 John 1:8–10.

"No temptation has overtaken you . . .": 1 Corinthians 10:13, NKJV.

"These things are written that you might not sin": 1 John 1:8–10.

Chapter Twenty-Nine. Love Your Father
In *Entertainment Weekly* (Sept. 24, 2004) Lucas was asked whether *Star Wars* wasn't really "a six-movie series about someone losing his humanity," and he replied, "But being resurrected by his children. We all have to make up for our fathers, you know" (p. 35).

Agape love is described in 1 Corinthians 13:4–7 (New Living Translation).

Paul Simon's "Slip Sliding Away" can be found on the Warner Brothers album *Negotiations and Love Songs 1971–1986.*

Vader's mask is taken off in *Star Wars: Episode VI. Return of the Jedi.*

"For you did not receive a spirit of slavery . . .": Romans 8:15.

Chapter Thirty. Make Your Masterpiece by Living It
"The spiritual life is about . . .": Parker Palmer, quoted in Mark Nepo's *The Book of Awakening* (York Beach, Maine: Conari Press, 2000).

The Talmud tells the story of Akiba on his deathbed.

"The kind of work God usually calls you to . . .": Frederick Buechner, *Wishful Thinking: A Theological ABC* (San Francisco: HarperSanFrancisco, revised and expanded edition, 1993).

"Worse than unbelievers": 1 Timothy 5:8.

Chapter Thirty-One. Loving, Transforming Presence
"God is love . . ." (1 John 4:8). God "so loved the world . . ." (John 3:16).

"Moved with compassion . . .": Matthew 9:36.

The story of the Pharisees and the adulterer is in John 8. "Go your way . . ." (John 8:11).

"The word became flesh . . .": John Rutter's music and the lyrics for St. Patrick's Prayer are from his 1988 Gloria (recorded on Collegium).

Chapter Thirty-Two. Counter Culture Like an Alien
For more on the Jedi Creed and Code, see Bill Slavicsek, A Guide to the Star Wars Universe (New York: Ballantine, 3rd edition, 2000).

On Jews arriving in America, see Ron Grossman's Sept. 14, 2004, Chicago Tribune article, "Jewish Americans Mark 350 Years of Diversity in an 'Open Society.'"

For more on the immigrant experience, see Mary Pipher, The Middle of Everywhere (Orlando, Fla.: Harcourt Brace, 2002).

For more on Modigliani, see the New York Times article "Modigliani: Plane Geometry Personalized," by Michael Kimmelman (May 21, 2004).

Sting's song "Englishman in New York" is on A&M's 2002 release *The Very Best of Sting and the Police.*

James Baldwin's comment is in a *New York Times* article, Sept. 13, 2004, "A Literary Friendship in Black and White: For James Baldwin and Sol Stein, Words Kindled a Fire."

For more on *ekklesia and koinonia,* see Gerhard Kittel's *A Theological Dictionary of the New Testament* (Grand Rapids, Mich.: Eerdmans, 1964); W. F. Arndt and F. W. Gingrich's *A Greek English Lexicon of the New Testament* (Chicago: University of Chicago Press, 1957); and Emil Brunner's *The Misunderstanding of the Church* (London: Lutterworth Press, 1952).

Stanley Haeurwas and William Willimon explore the church's alternative community in *Resident Aliens: Life in the Christian Colony* (Nashville, Tenn.: Abingdon Press, 1989).

Ernest Hemingway's reference to Paris is found in *A Moveable Feast* (New York: Scribner, 1996).

Peter's advice to counter culture like an alien is in 1 Peter 2:11, 2:12, and 3:15–16.

Chapter Thirty-Three. Better World, Better Way

For a complete description of Jedi use of the Force, see Bill Slavicsek, *A Guide to the Star Wars Universe* (New York: Ballantine, 3rd edition, 2000).

"So God created humankind . . .": Genesis 1:26–28.

"Go therefore and make disciples . . .": Matthew 28:19–20.

Genesis 4:20–22 follows the progression of industry ("Zillah bore Tubal-cain. . . .").

"A Christian, above all . . .": Edith Schaeffer, *The Hidden Art of Homemaking* (Lowestoft, U.K.: Tyndale House, 1985).

See *USA Today,* Oct. 16, 2002, for the Carlos Santana comment.

Paul described the followers of Jesus as diverse yet unified in Galatians 3:28.

Karl Rahner (1904–1984) has been called the most influential Catholic theologian of the twentieth century. One of the hallmarks of Rahner's Christian faith was his belief that "a person can experience God's very own self." See Harvey D. Egan's *Karl Rahner: The Mystic of Everyday Life* (New York: Crossroad, 1998).

The Brennan Manning comment is from a *Dick Staub Show* interview on Dec. 9, 2003, when we discussed his book, *Ruthless Trust* (San Francisco: HarperSanFrancisco, 2002).

From a *Dick Staub Show* interview with Thomas Steinbeck on his book *Down to a Soundless Sea* (New York: Ballantine, 2002).

Chapter Thirty-Four. Preserve, Repair, and Make Beautiful
St. Bonaventure on St. Francis is quoted on-line at http://www.chebucto.ns.ca/Religion/SFO/patron.html.

"I do not think of all the misery . . .": Anne Frank, in her journal, *Anne Frank: The Diary of a Young Girl* (New York: Bantam, 1993; first published in 1947).

Chapter Thirty-Five. Live Simply, Pack Light, Hold Loose
For more on affluenza, see the book by that title (San Francisco: Berrett-Koehler, 2002), edited by John De Graaf.

"Empty-handed we came into the world . . .": 1 Timothy 6:7–10.

"Experience shows that it is an easy thing . . .": Richard Mather, *Farewell Sermon.* Cited in Randy Alcorn's *Money, Possessions and Eternity* (Wheaton, Ill.: Tyndale House, 2003).

"Seek God's kingdom first" (Matthew 6:33). "Where your treasure is . . ." (Matthew 6:21). "It will be hard for a rich person . . ." (Matthew 19:23).

"I have just three things to teach . . ." is from Lao-Tzu, *Tao Te Ching.* "Live simply . . ." is a quote from Mahatma Gandhi that is found on-line in multiple places, including http://www.americancatholic.org/Newsletters/YU/ay0503.asp. "Because they had nothing . . ." is from Thomas Celano, *First Life of St. Francis* (London: Society for Promoting Christian Knowledge, 2000).

"If everyone would take . . .": St. Basil, quoted at http://www.streetlevel.ca/biographies/St_Francis2002.htm.

"I left no money to anyone . . .": John Wesley, *The*

Journal of John Wesley, ed. Percy Livingstone Parker (Chicago: Moody Press, 1951), p. 409.

"To have what we want is riches . . .": George MacDonald, quoted in Richard Foster's *Freedom of Simplicity* (San Francisco: HarperSanFrancisco, 1981).

Chapter Thirty-Six. The Least of These

The United Nations statistics come from the Millenium Indicators Report on-line at http://millenniumindicators.un.org/unsd/mi/mi_goals.asp.

U.S. Department of Labor Statistics are available on-line at http://www.bls.gov/.

"The Spirit of the Lord is upon me . . .": Luke 4:18.

"The blind receive their sight . . .": Luke 7:22.

"Jesus made it frighteningly clear . . .": Matthew 25:31–46.

"When the Son of Man . . . ": Matthew 25:31–40.

"Let this mind be in you . . .": Philippians 2:5.

"Whoever has two coats . . .": Luke 3:11.

Chapter Thirty-Seven. Pursue God in the Company of Friends

In his famous Meditation XVII, the metaphysical poet John Donne said "no man is an island." Paul Simon's "I Am a Rock" is on Simon and Garfunkel's 1966 Sony album *Sounds of Silence.* The Eagles' "Desperado" is the title song from the Elektra/Asylum album of 1990.

"Christ has no body . . .": St. Teresa's Prayer is listed on the following Web site: http://elvis.rowan.edu/~kilroy/JEK/query.cgi?10+15b. The Web site also includes a biography of St. Teresa.

"I have no need of you": 1 Corinthians 12.

Chapter Thirty-Eight. Forgive, Forgive, and Again Forgive

"Father, forgive them . . .": Luke 23:24.

The story about the Serbian woman on CNN is told by Nevada Barr in *Seeking Enlightenment Hat by Hat* (New York: Berkley Books, 2003).

Karl Barth's comment on gratitude is quoted in a *Chris-*

tian Century review of the book *Before God* by George Stroup (Grand Rapids, Mich.: Eerdmans, 2004).

In *Prayers of the Martyrs* (Grand Rapids, Mich.: Zondervan, 1991), we read about the note found in a dead child's coat at the Ravensbruck concentration camp.

Chapter Thirty-Nine. In Age Is Opportunity
The familiar poem "Crabbed Age and Youth," written in 1599, is generally attributed to Shakespeare (*Oxford Book of English Verse: 1250–1900*); Sir Arthur Quiller-Couch, ed.; Oxford, England: Oxford University Press, 1939).

"In the last days . . .": Acts 2:17.

"Let no one despise your youth . . . " (1 Timothy 4:12). "In the same way, you who are younger . . ." (1 Peter 5:5).

"Lording it over the flock" and "setting an example": 1 Peter 5:1–4.

"I am writing to you . . .": 1 John 2:13–14.

Chapter Forty. Another Chance
"A man after God's own heart . . .": 1 Samuel 13:13–14, New International Version.

Read about David's adultery and murder of Uriah in 2 Samuel, chapters 9–12.

"Have mercy on me, O God . . .": Psalm 51.

Chapter Forty-One. Touch the Sky
"Do you not know that in a race . . ." (1 Corinthians 9:24–27). "Let us lay aside every weight . . ." (Hebrews 12:1).

"His roots sank deep . . .": Mark 4:3–8.

Jesus and the metaphor of the vine and branches: John 15:1–6.

"Some persons of a scientific turn . . .": Kathleen Norris, *Amazing Grace* (New York: Riverhead, 1998).

"One of the few things I know about writing . . .": Annie Dillard, *The Writing Life* (New York: HarperPerennial, reprint edition, 1990).

"Fight the good fight of faith . . ." (1 Timothy 1:19 and 1 Timothy 6:1). "As for me . . ." (2 Timothy 4:7).

John Rutter's music and the lyrics for the Gaelic prayer are from his 1988 *Gloria* (Collegium).

Mike Yaconelli, *Messy Spirituality* (Grand Rapids, Mich.: Zondervan, 2002).

"Now the God of peace . . .": Hebrews 13:20–21.

THE AUTHOR

D ick Staub is a broadcaster, writer, and speaker whose work focuses on interpreting faith and culture. The director of the Center for Faith and Culture and adjunct professor at Seattle Pacific University, he is also the radio personality behind the *Dick Staub Show,* an award-winning, nationally syndicated daily broadcast he hosted for fifteen years. Dick's interviews are a popular feature on

Christianity Today's website, and his daily blog (dickstaub.com) draws thousands of visitors each month. He serves on the board of *Image: A Journal of Religion & the Arts* and plays a strategic role in the C. S. Lewis Foundation.

A New Kind of Christian: A Tale of Two Friends on a Spiritual Journey

Brian D. McLaren

Hardcover
ISBN: 0–7879–5599–X

Winner of the *Christianity Today* Award of Merit for Best Christian Living Title, 2002

"This is a book that heightens the depths and deepens the peaks. Like all the best things in life, it is not to be entered into lightly, but reverently and in the fear of a God who is waiting for the church to stop asking WWJD, 'What would Jesus do?' and start asking WIJD, 'What is Jesus doing?'"
—Dr. Leonard Sweet, E. Stanley Jones Chair of Evangelism at Drew University, founder and president of SpiritVenture Ministries, and best-selling author

BRIAN D. MCLAREN is the founding pastor of Cedar Ridge Community Church in the Washington-Baltimore area and the author of acclaimed books on contemporary Christianity, including *The Church on the Other Side: Doing Ministry in the Postmodern Matrix* (2000), and the following trilogy from Jossey-Bass: *A New Kind of Christian, The Story We Find Ourselves In,* and *The Last Word and the Word After That.*

*My Faith So Far:
A Story of Conversion
and Confusion*

Patton Dodd

Hardcover
ISBN: 0–7879–6859–5

"The power of this memoir is how well Dodd captures the messiness of faith. . . ."
—Lauren Winner, for *Christianity Today*; author, *Girl Meets God*

"In an engaging writing style that allows him to be both protagonist and dispassionate observer, Dodd stands outside himself and, with insight and humor, presents a young man's search for God, piety, and the answers to all life's imponderables."
—Donna Chavez, *Booklist*

"This lively coming-of-age story succeeds both as literary memoir and as an intimate look at a popular variety of American religious experience."
—*Publishers Weekly*

PATTON DODD is a writer and editor living in Boston, Massachusetts. Patton has written for both religious and general audiences, including *re:generation quarterly, Christianity Today, Colorado Springs Independent, Life@Work,* as well as numerous webzines. He is a doctoral candidate in religion and literature at Boston University.